I WENT TO SCHOOL ... IN THE JUNGLE

Books by the same author:

THE SHARK'S FIN FIVE
TARA
MY BOOK ABOUT HUDSON

I went to school ...
...in the jungle

Sheila Miller

OMF BOOKS

JF
F
mil

© OVERSEAS MISSIONARY FELLOWSHIP

First published in the United Kingdom 1975
Reprinted   1979
Reprinted   1981
Reprinted in Singapore   1997

Acknowledgements
Cover by Jonathan Neil Miller
Line drawings by the Chefoo children
Poems on page 87 by Mark Yand and
Andrew Davis

ISBN 0 85363 109 3

Made in Great Britain
Published by the Overseas Missionary Fellowship,
Belmont, The Vine, Sevenoaks, Kent TN13 3TZ, and
printed by Stanley L. Hunt (Printers) Ltd, Midland
Road, Rushden, Northants NN10 9UA

Heavenly Father,
thank you
for
Toots,
Stella,
Fish,
Aunty Janet
and Miss Summers
who
represent Your world-wide
Chefoo family
of which I'm glad to
be
a part.

CONTENTS

CONTENTS

1

GOODBYE

'Where are we?' My small voice was bewildered as I found myself suddenly shaken awake by the lurching Mercedes.

'On the last lap of our journey to school!'

'What time is it?'

'Midnight.'

Midnight to arrive at the school in the jungle!

We snaked on in our train of taxis. Twenty-four huge headlights lit the trees by the side of the road. Jungle trees! Were there any tigers?

'Yes!'

'Snakes?' I asked, trembling with excitement.

'Yes! Pit vipers, yellow bellies, mountain racers, banded crites . . .'

'Monkeys?'

'Oh yes!'

'Eleph . . .'

But then I saw the gateposts of the school—CHEFOO School.

School! I was sent to school. So were you, of course, but my school was a *boarding* school and I went there when I was only five.

As my mother is Irish, she named me Teresa, but I'm never called that now. Actually I rejoice in the full name of Teresa Olivia Odetta Thrower. Dreadful, isn't it? No wonder I was glad when my friends called me Toots. T for Teresa, O for Olivia, O for Odetta and T for Thrower. Get it? I'm not sure where the 's' comes in! My friends started it but now even my mother seldom comes out with 'Teresa'. The only time I ever vaguely liked that name was when we did a French play at school and I was Thérèse. I felt I had a sort of fellow-feeling there.

School! Yes, that's what I was going to tell you about. I was really excited that first day—the day I left home. I had heard about my school almost as soon as I'd learnt to listen. To be big enough to go to school was what I longed for. I was thoroughly prepared for the adventure and quite happy to say goodbye to Mum and Dad.

In the future there were days when I missed them very badly, when life seemed unbearable without them, when I was so homesick that I wanted to go back to Thailand— but that *first* day was an exciting adventure for me. My parents were really astonished to see that I couldn't get away quickly enough!

What a journey it was! My Mum and Dad work in North Thailand—up in the mountains, among the tribal people called the Méo. The trip to school was 1,500 miles long! One and a half thousand miles didn't mean anything to me. School in Malaysia was only a far-off field which was green and inviting. Later I learned that the great distance meant an awful lot to Mum and Dad. Although there were no tears in *my* eyes, there were in Mum's. She stood at Chiang Mai's little airport, blinking and waving as her five-year-old boarded the Thai Airways plane.

The first lap of my journey took me right down to Bangkok. I travelled with a teacher from school and five

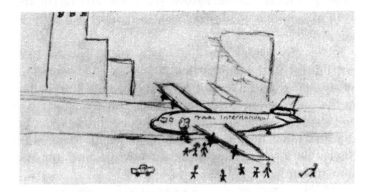

. . . her five-year-old boarded the Thai Airways plane.

other Chefusians. Our school is called Chefoo (pronounced Cheefoo) after a port in China, where the first Chefoo school was, a long time ago. When the missionaries had to leave China, our school moved right down to Malaysia in south-east Asia. They left China behind but they didn't leave the name. Although we were now to live in the Cameron Highlands we were still known as Chefusians from Chefoo School.

Bangkok was big and bustling. The teacher, a pretty auburn-haired lady called Miss Summers, herded us into our Guest House. Kids were running about all over the place, because all the children from Thailand were gathering there before beginning the long trip to school. I was thrilled. I forgot all about Chiang Mai airport. I forgot all about our little Méo mountain village. I even forgot about Mum and Dad. I let go of Miss Summers' hand and bounded across the lawn to the swing.

That night I slept in the big noisy Guest House. The traffic rumbled through Bangkok's streets, but I didn't hear it. Hours in the garden, romping around in the tropical sunshine, had taken their toll and I was dead to the world.

Stella slept beside me that night. Stella was the first girl I'd met in the garden that afternoon. She wanted to swing and so did I. We took turns and became firm friends in the space of one short hour. Stella was six—just six—and she too was going to Chefoo School in Malaysia for the first time. In fact, my new name Toots began with Stella that lovely August night when we dreamed our way into adventure.

The big part of our adventurous journey to school started the next afternoon. Miss Summers and two other teachers from Chefoo School bustled every one of us into two buses. Mums and dads were there too, packing cases and trunks into the luggage-compartments. Our number had grown to 67! All the Chefoo children who lived in Thailand were getting ready for the mammoth train journey which would take us far away from Bangkok, right down into Malaysia.

Two coaches on the train had been reserved for our party. Stella and I found a big cushioned, comfortable seat each. Some big kids pushed past our legs to stand at the window. They were the ones who lived in Bangkok and were now saying goodbye to *their* mums and dads. One tall girl with long blonde hair quite suddenly began to sob. I was surprised. I thought big girls like that didn't cry. I watched her dabbing at her red eyes with a hankie. Then I noticed a boy crying. He was quite big too. He stood by the next window with his hand out, holding on to his dad. I saw his dad reach a little parcel into the boy's hand. The whistle blew. The train lurched. It moved and slowly gathered speed. The platform began to slip away. The waving mums and dads were left behind.

Suddenly I was aware of all sorts of rustling of paper. It was time to open goodbye presents. Do you know what? I decided to bawl then as well! It wasn't because I wanted my Mum and Dad—it was because I wanted a goodbye present too! I forgot that I had said goodbye the day before and had had a big box of sweets to munch on the plane!

Stella, my new good friend, gave me a kick. It was quite a sore kick! For a moment I thought of bawling louder but Stella, even from that early age, was gifted with sound common sense.

'Shut up!' she said. I thought it was *very* rude. I wasn't allowed to say 'shut up' at home. However, it had the needed effect. I stopped crying and began to look around once more.

Miss Summers was flitting up and down the aisle between the seats. Calmly and efficiently she was dealing with those Chefusians who were still sobbing. Out came a big box of comics. It was followed by another box full of colouring books and pencils. Keeping us amused had begun.

Twenty-four hours that journey took. The clean, spruce children who had boarded that train came off a day later a filthy mess! We had eaten there, slept there, tried to wash there, fought there and read there. We'd even written a letter home. All I did was a drawing, of course, but Miss Summers said she would put it in an envelope and send it home to Mum and Dad. It was a specially good drawing, I thought. I'd sketched the train with all its rows of windows, and me looking out at the paddy fields.

Thai trains are modern, but Miss Summers didn't think

they were germ-free! She kept telling us to wash our hands. If the tops of our water bottles fell on the floor, they had to be washed too. Every meal time she washed the table tops. All the food was in big boxes. It had all been prepared in the Bangkok Guest House—hundreds of sandwiches! That was the day I took a liking to peanut butter, and I've loved it ever since.

It wasn't until late the next afternoon that we reached a town called Butterworth in the north of Malaysia. What a shuffle! We all had to get off, *and* all our luggage. Was I glad! I was far too hot with the tropical sun burning in through the window.

The heat was still intense on the station platform—just as bad as Bangkok, I thought, but Bangkok was many hundreds of miles away now.

At last we were ready to leave the station. I noticed for the first time that five grown-ups were with us. Somebody's mum and dad had travelled with the party. An Indian man came up to Miss Summers with a box. After delving into it, she began handing out sweaters to everyone! I couldn't imagine what we needed sweaters for. I took one anyway, but I didn't put it on. I was far too hot and sticky and dirty.

The Indian man was a taxi driver. A whole row of taxis was lined up outside the station. They had all come from the Cameron Highlands to take us to Chefoo School. Miss Summers began sorting us out, and Stella and I were shoved in together in Taxi Number Twelve. That was the last taxi, and Miss Summers got in too.

I don't remember much about that part of the long journey. It seemed to me that we were speeding along Malaysia's highways just about for ever. At one point we were given a bag of food and I found another peanut butter sandwich. I think that was when I fell asleep, with my head bumping on Miss Summers' shoulder. And then I was suddenly awake again. It was dark and surprisingly cold. No soft warm air was flooding the taxi now. Miss Summers had leant forward and was closing a window. I shivered. But I learned just then that we'd reached the mountains and our long journey was nearly over.

'Put on your sweater, Teresa,' Miss Summers continued after explaining about the wild life of the jungle.

I struggled in the cramped back seat of the taxi. My legs had gone to sleep and I had a horrible attack of pins and needles. I tried to stand up.

'Careful!' warned Miss Summers. 'Watch Stella!'

And there was Stella MacAlpine asleep on the floor!

Quite suddenly I didn't feel the least bit sleepy any more. The air was clear. The moon peeped out from behind the clouds. The taxi was flooded with its pale light.

Through the night we had jolted on and on. The mountain road had wound up and up, in and out. Now that I was awake, I was aware that I had been thrown from side to side every few moments as the taxi lurched round yet another bend. Ugh!

'Nearly there,' whispered Miss Summers. We had passed the gateposts and were following the other eleven taxis round the dark drive. We turned the corner and there was the school—all brightly lit in the dark and as welcoming as could be!

The playground became a mass of crumpled sleepy forms, getting out of the taxis. I saw a nice-looking lady coming over to us.

'Are you Teresa?' she asked, taking me by the hand.

I nodded. 'And that's Stella on the floor,' I pointed.

I stepped out on to Chefoo ground. The jerky, twisting taxi journey suddenly had an unwanted result. Promptly and violently, I was sick!

2

POISON!

Jumbled together in my memory are all the events of those first packed weeks at Chefoo. Everything was new. All was strange. Except for the few older children from North Thailand, I knew nobody—nobody, that is, except Stella and Miss Summers.

In spite of the strangeness, I was happy. I found another new friend in my dorm aunty. Poor lady! Her first introduction to Teresa Olivia Odetta Thrower was rather unfortunate and completely ruined her good, navy, leather shoes! However, she soon cleaned me, herself and the playground up, and as quickly as could be had her four little newcomers from Thailand bathed and tucked up in bed sipping a hot chocolate drink.

One great mercy of my life is that I *never* have any bother sleeping. It saves quite a few complications! That night I again fell asleep as soon as my head touched the pillow. That was the pattern for many nights to come. I never heard the muffled sobs from other beds at seven o'clock, but our new dorm aunty did. She was always there.

Our new dorm aunty was plump and cuddly. We called her Aunty Eva. She came from Canada. Aunty Eva had a huge doll's house waiting for us in Dorm 7. We loved that house. We spring-cleaned it every day of the week. It helped us to forget about homesickness and loneliness.

One of the dorm uncles was marvellous at painting. He painted a large mural on our west wall. It was a Hansel and Gretel house. At night I used to go to sleep facing the two houses—the big doll's one and the pink sugary one on the wall. Aunty Eva would creep about in the twilight, whispering goodnight and giving last-minute hugs.

Our teacher was from Australia.

'Put your books on the tyble,' she would say. Or, 'It's taime to go for bryke and have a sendwich!'

At first I could hardly make out what she meant when she spoke. I kept saying 'Pardon?' in a British-Thai-Irish accent, and the Americans in our class just said, 'What?' To say 'What?' isn't rude in America, like it is in Britain, but now that I'm twelve I have the greatest difficulty remembering which customs belong to which country. I mean, when I go home to Britain, is it correct to eat with your fork in your left hand or your right? I cringe when I think of the time I copied the Méo, at Grandma's table. They eat with their fingers—a handy habit!

Everything at Chefoo was going fine—until one day towards the end of my first term. Something awful happened. It caused a big stir at Chefoo, and though I was still very young (six years and two months to be exact), I remember vividly what happened.

John and Maurice were kicking a ball about on the playing field. Feeling full of beans, John gave the ball a hefty whack. It sailed up in the air and descended out of sight behind the headmaster's house.

'Jumpin' Jemima! That's done it!' yelled John.

'You silly nit. You can just go up after it,' ordered Maurice.

'But . . .'

'Oh, come on! I'll go with you.'

'It's out of bounds,' John protested feebly.

'It'll only take us a minute. Come on! No one's about.'

Daringly the boys climbed the bank behind the headmaster's house. No sign of the ball. And then Maurice thought he saw a splodge of red showing among the tall grass at the jungle's edge. He climbed higher and nearer.

'Got it!' he yelled.

John too leapt off the bank.

Unknown to the boys, a deadly pit viper lay hidden in the undergrowth. Maurice's flying leap landed right on the vicious creature's tail. It reared to strike, but Maurice had run out of danger. It was John who was bitten. Following in his friend's tracks, he too leapt off the bank. Steadying himself by his hands on the ground, he was an easy target for the angry reptile. It got him just between the thumb and first finger. A v-shaped, tell-tale mark showed where the poison had gone in. John yelled—partly in pain and partly in fear: 'Maurice, Maurice help! A snake! It's got me!'

Maurice hesitated only a moment. To get help was more important than sneaking back safely to the playing field. He bounded down the bank shouting for Aunty Kay, whom he knew was on duty in the playground.

John dragged himself slowly after him. His hand was beginning to swell. He knew that fatal results often followed snake-bite. Vaguely he wondered if these were his last minutes on earth. He'd reached the corner of the building now. He held on to the solid brick with his one good hand. Just before he collapsed, he saw Aunty Kay racing towards him, a motley crowd of boys and girls in play shorts bounding behind.

Aunty Kay picked John up in her arms. This was some feat, because John was in the top class—a big, hefty eleven-year-old.

'The school nurse!' she panted. 'Run, Maurice! Get Aunty Mary!'

The tension was heightened when Aunty Mary couldn't be found; and, to make matters worse, she was out in the school van.

Fortunately Aunty Kay herself was a trained nurse. Rather frantically she tied a tourniquet on John's arm to try to prevent the poison from circulating round his body.

'We must get him to the clinic in Tanah Rata,' she said. Tanah Rata was the little mountain town four miles away.

Uncle Ted was found, and like magic his little old car

came chugging along the drive to pick John up. Aunty Kay said afterwards that the drive to the clinic seemed never ending. At last, however, John had an injection of anti-snake-bite serum.

The weeks that followed were tense. John was rushed down the long, winding mountain road to hospital in Ipoh, 70 miles away. For three days he hovered between life and death. Aunty Mary had gone with him, and for those three days she sat with him day and night. His mother and father were called for—all the way from Indonesia. The whole school was sobered

In our dorm all of us girls prayed hard every night and morning for John's life. We really meant it. We prayed. We needed to. John lay there in hospital day after day, still dangerously ill. We prayed and God heard.

John lived. Never again would he or any other one of us dare to play in the jungle. In no uncertain terms the headmaster outlined once again our play boundaries. After weeks of worry, John's mother and father were able to go home. Three weeks passed before John was able to come up to school again. After all that time, his arm was still swollen.

Why didn't John die? Young though I was, a new and important aspect of Chefoo life was dawning on me. Here we were—an assortment of 100 primary school children from all over south-east Asia—hidden away in a little valley among Malaysia's jungle-covered mountains.

But we were never hidden from God's eyes. Do you know what I think? I believe that His angel stood in Chefoo grounds—tall and magnificent, a warrior, keeping us safe. Otherwise, how could it be that there are so few dangerous accidents? Out of all the snake bites that we could have had, there was only that one all the time I was at Chefoo, and the Lord did not allow it to be fatal.

'Snake! A snake in the grass!' The cry sometimes rings out several times a week, *but* the Bible verse that says, 'The angel of the Lord encamps around those who fear Him, and delivers them,' is absolutely true.

3

THE POP-DRINKING PONY

Of course, snakes weren't the only creatures we had at Chefoo. Once upon a time there was Pete. Pete was our pony, but he was no ordinary horse, for Pete enjoyed a good drink of pop, he liked ice-cream, and he loved to watch TV.

It's not every day of your life you come across a pony like that. Our headmaster thought he was rather unusual when *he* heard about him.

'How much will this pony cost to buy?' he asked, slightly concerned.

'We'd be glad to *give* Pete to you', his owner replied, 'in return for Pete having a good home.'

'His home would be a school,' our head said, '—a school with 100 children! Do you think . . . ?'

'Oh, yes,' replied Mrs Marsh. She was a comfortable-looking lady, and was truly anxious to find a good home for Pete. 'I'm getting old now,' she confided. 'Pete needs somebody younger to look after him. Besides, it's so hot down in the plains where I live. Pete will thrive in the cool mountain air!'

Our head had one or two question marks still in his mind. Pete lived many miles away—far beyond the bottom of our mountain road which itself was 40 miles long. How on earth could Pete be brought up the mountain?

Uncle Ted, the artistic one, at last came up with an idea. He was used to animals, he said. He grew up on a farm in the States. Why not send down the old school van for the pony? All that needed doing was to have the seats removed, and he would string a cradle to support the horse in the space left.

Hmm!

But wasn't it worth it? Imagine! A pony for nothing! So Uncle Ted made the long, long journey to Pete's home.

Everything worked according to plan. I'll never, in all my life, forget the morning Pete came to Chefoo. I was in my second year then. Leaving home was harder now, but my love for my school was growing.

That first morning that we children saw Pete was a Sunday. We all knew a surprise was in the offing, because the big old school bell had rung, and it wasn't even church time.

There we stood in groups on the netball court, wondering what we were there for. Suddenly somebody happened to glance down the valley, beyond the playing field. Uncle Ted was riding up towards the pitch—on a horse!

That was the first time we saw dear old chestnut-coloured Pete. Uncle Ted raised his hand high in the air—for all the world like a cowboy—and yelled, 'He's yours, kids. This is Pete and he belongs to you!'

Uncle Ted raised his hand high in the air—for all the world like a cowboy.

Nobody wanted to go to church that Sunday!

Imagine our delight, the next morning, when Pete appeared at morning prayers in the school assembly hall! We had just sung *Negara ku*, the Malaysian National Anthem, when our headmaster drew back the heavy red stage curtains. There sat Uncle Ted on Pete! I never heard of a horse being at school prayers before, or since!

Uncle Ted demonstrated then how to handle Pete. He showed us his harness, he showed us how to put the saddle and bridle on, the correct way to approach him, how to hand him sugar lumps, and best of all, how to mount him. Sally volunteered to try that. She was one of the big girls, and she hopped right into the saddle with no trouble at all. How I *envied* her!

It was a good assembly that day. And that was the day, too, that Pony Club began. I was the very first girl to write my name down on the entry list, and I soon discovered my Pony Club time would be on Tuesdays at 6.15.

I could hardly wait! On Tuesday after supper Stella and I wandered away down the valley by the stream to Pete's Pasture. Uncle Ted was there. He was painting a notice on the little shed where Pete was going to live. It said 'Pete's Palace'. Then he led Pete slowly and carefully up to the playing fields. After he had exercised him a bit, it was our dorm's turn for rides.

Oh—the thrill of mounting Pete for the first time. Uncle Ted walked me up the playing field, and I had visions of myself becoming a great show-jumper or something else regal that went with this tremendous feeling of being on a horse!

A memorable day! But unfortunately I have another memory of that evening—not quite so pleasant—for that was the day, too, that a little niggling annoyance grew into something big. The trouble was in human form. She was Abigail Fischer. She was big. She was seven. She was in my dorm, and she was in my class.

Of all the things that have happened to me at Chefoo School, Abigail Fischer has been the worst. Talk about a strong will! Everything just had to go her way. And talk about a loud voice! She just shouted every one of us down. She was always jumping up and down round Aunty Eva and forever sticking her hand up in class, looking for the teacher's attention. It didn't take me until my second year at Chefoo to know I didn't like her. But until that wonderful day when I rode Pete for the first time, we'd never had a stand-up row.

And there I was, on Pete's back for the very first time, feeling like a princess, when Abigail Fischer came running down to the playing field.

'It's my turn now,' she announced to Uncle Ted and

me, and taking hold of poor Pete's bridle she gave it a great tug.

The princess feeling vanished. Everybody was allowed to ride the length of the playing field and back, and I was only half-way back.

'Let go, you great fish,' I shouted, more loudly than I meant to. Fish's mother called her 'Gail', but I never did. I thought it was too nice for her.

'Teresa!' Uncle Ted exclaimed. I nearly fell off old Pete. Uncle Ted never called me Teresa. I knew then that I'd annoyed him.

'Well,' I defended myself, 'she's always barging in and it's *not* her turn—not for two more minutes anyway. Spiteful little brat!'

Uncle Ted put his arms round my waist and lifted me straight off Pete.

'Teresa, until you learn to speak nicely to your friends, you'll have to do with short rides only,' he said.

'*She's* not my friend,' I exploded. 'Who would want that . . . that . . . that *fish* for a friend?'

But no one was listening. Uncle Ted lifted Abigail Fischer on to Pete and let her have *my* ride to the end of the playing field. There she sat, looking down her freckly, pimply nose at me and smirking.

Oh, I was *so* mad. I ran up the bank from the field, past everyone who was watching, and up to Aunty Eva's room. Hot angry tears were streaming down my face, and I choked back big, racking sobs.

'Listen, little Toots,' came Aunty Eva's soft voice. 'This kind of thing happens to everybody. There are *always* people we find hard to get on with. But we must learn to take them as they are. Gail has to learn to like you, too, and she'll have a hard job if you show as much temper as that over such a small thing.'

'It's *not* a small thing,' I stormed. 'She's stolen my ride! I'll never forgive her.'

And it took me a long time to do so.

But my stormy interview with Abigail didn't stop me enjoying dear old Pete. I learnt to handle him properly. I learnt to walk round his back quietly so as not to frighten him. I learnt how to ride through an obstacle course when Uncle Ted planted little flags on the playing field. I even learnt how to ride up and down the bank round the field, and I was one of the enthusiasts who helped Uncle Ted to feed him every day. I just loved that animal.

You can imagine, then, the distress I felt when one day, one much-looked-forward-to Tuesday, Uncle Ted said we couldn't ride him.

'Why?'

'Why?'

'Why?' we chorused, disappointed and worried.

Uncle Ted was obviously at a loss for words.

'Is he sick?' I asked, jumping to a conclusion.

'Well, he might be,' said Uncle Ted. 'One thing for sure is, that he's a very *old* horse. I think he can't take your weight any longer.'

'Oh, just let me try,' I pleaded in desperation.

Uncle Ted took us down to Pete's Pasture. The old pony was looking miserably out of his little palace.

'Come here, Pete, old boy,' said Uncle Ted gently.

He lifted me on to his back. Although Uncle Ted was still supporting some of my seven-year-old weight, I felt the pony's back sag beneath me.

'You see,' said Uncle Ted sadly. 'He's buckling at the knees.'

That was an awful shock to us all. Nobody after that asked for another ride. We knew it would be cruel to the old pony.

From then on, it was only memories—memories of that first ride, memories of how we'd learnt to handle a horse, memories of half term when Pete had been dressed up for a special occasion with his mane and tail braided and ribbons in his hair.

Somehow we knew that Pete wouldn't last long. And we were right. Just three months after Pete came to join our Chefoo family, he died. He died in a gentle, peaceful sort of way, for our school doctor thought it best to 'put him to sleep'. Afterwards Uncle Ted and our Indian gardener buried Pete down by the stream—just beyond his special little palace. His bones are still there.

That night there was hardly a dry pillow at Chefoo School. Nobody seemed to understand why *our* special pony had to die. Where was he now? Was there an animal heaven? Why did God let it happen?

When the first flurry of tears was brushed away, we began to see that Pete just had to die because of old age. This was one of the facts of life. Old animals and old people die. God never really planned His beautiful world that way. Aunty Eva said that Satan was the one responsible for death. She said that the whole of God's creation was out of gear because of Satan and sin. Gathering us girls round her, she opened her Bible and read to us—read to us about a day that was coming when people won't die any more, and when animals will be happy too. Even animal enemies, like a lion and a lamb, will be able to lie down together and sleep peacefully beside each other.

Our thoughts were turned from the tragedy of Pete's death to the loving plans God had made for the future. One day Satan would be locked up and everyone would be happy with King Jesus reigning.

These ideas comforted us quite a bit, but all the same, I wonder if there will be horses in heaven?

4

DISASTER!

The intercom buzzed, loud and clear, in the Head's house. He leapt out of bed and dashed to answer it in his pyjamas. Who was ringing so early in the morning—holiday time, too.

'Yes?' questioned Mr M sharply. (M stands for Melville, but he seldom gets his full name.)

Silence at his end. Then an astonished gasp.

'What?' he exclaimed. 'Did you say a classroom wall, Anna? What classroom? A classroom wall—*caved in*?'

Down went the receiver with a bang. On went the Head's clothes—on top of his pyjamas. Dashing out of the house, he didn't even pause to grab a raincoat, although it was one of the few mornings when the Cameron Highlands was *not* bright and sunny.

What a sight met his eyes! It was true! The wall of Room 3 was *in* the classroom. So was the huge window frame *and* a few tons of bright orange mountainside. The hill behind the school had slipped during the night and a landslide in the classroom met Mr M's horrified gaze.

Into the bargain, the heavy fall of soil had fractured a water pipe. Murky orange water gushed everywhere. Our textbooks from the overturned bookcase floated out of the classroom door on a muddy tide. Just think of it! If *only* I had been there to see it. . . . Can you imagine a happier sight than twenty maths books floating away down the corridor?

There seemed nothing else for it—the Head tore off his shoes and socks, rolled up his trouser legs (both pairs), grabbed a broom and, with the help of other staff members, began to sweep out the muddy mess.

That, you may think, would put paid to a new term starting in a few weeks' time. Well you're wrong. We went to school as usual, but it wasn't *ordinary* school. This was *interesting* school, and here's what happened.

That school year I was eight years old, and had moved to Level 3. That was the year, too, that Patrick came to Chefoo.

Patrick is my young brother. He's ten now, and a proper pest but, at that time, I was really proud of him. I used to lead him by the hand round all my favourite haunts in the Chefoo grounds.

With Patrick coming to school, it hadn't been quite so hard to leave Mum and Dad. As usual, Mum had handed us special goodbye presents at Chiang Mai airport.

'Don't open them till the plane takes off,' she said, smiling through the tears she was so desperately trying not to cry.

As I boarded the aircraft, I had the big parcel under my

arm. It felt soft and lumpy. I cut my waving short, as I tore frantically at the string!

Clothes!

A parcel of clothes! But these clothes weren't like anything you've ever seen before. It was the traditional outfit of the Méo tribespeople! I'd always wanted to dress like them, for I loved our little Méo village, our shack of a house and the fun Patrick and I had on the wooded hills round our home. We'd made good friends, too, with some of the Méo children, and both of us could chatter to them in their own language.

And now I'd be able to be like a little Méo girl myself! I was thrilled! I wanted to hop off the plane and give Mum such a special hug, but we were already getting ready to taxi down the runway. I had to content myself with waving the trousers of the outfit at the porthole window, stretching across a fat Thai lady to do so!

Flight or no flight, I just had to try on my new clothes. I pulled the black trousers over my jeans, fixed the beautifully-embroidered top and set the red apron in place. I could just imagine myself playing at Chefoo in my lovely tribal costume.

'Little girl, what *are* you doing?' It was the gorgeous Thai air hostess, racing down the aisle towards me. 'You must sit down. You must fasten your seat belt. We are about to take off! Woof!'

I came back to the present with a bump—a literal one, because the plane had started to taxi down the runway and the sudden speed threw me off my feet. I scrambled up, conscious that all the Thai passengers with their slanting eyes were intrigued with the little pale-skinned foreigner balancing in the air, in tribal costume!

A little note from Mum had fallen on the seat. I was glad to concentrate on deciphering it!

'When you wear your tribal outfit you can think of the Méo girls,' Mum had written. 'Perhaps your friends in the dorm would like to hear about Mahlee, and how she wants to believe in the Christian way but her parents won't let her.

'Lots of love to my darling Toots, and don't forget to keep half an eye on wee Patrick! Mum and Dad. XXXX'

Often, in the days to come, I'd be adjusting my tribal 'uniform' after school, and the thought of Mahlee would pop into my head. Her father planted opium and smoked it. Her mother worshipped the spirits. Would Mahlee ever be able to believe in Jesus? It would be so hard for her to grow up a Christian. Yet her life, as it was, would be even harder. How scared the Méo were of evil spirits. I shivered as I thought of it. In some ways I was glad to get back to the atmosphere of Chefoo School.

At the time I whole-heartedly agreed with all that my parents were doing. I just took it for granted that Patrick and I had to be sent to school. We couldn't grow up illiterate in a Méo village. It wasn't until I was twelve and had to stay in England at school that I began to think more about what it involved to be a missionary.

Returning to Chefoo after eight long weeks of holiday always brought surprises, but news of this landslide was the biggest we ever had.

In the dead of night we arrived as usual. Imagine our shock to see mounds of sand all over our play area.

'Aunty Janet!' Stella and I yelled (we'd graduated to the middle-sized-girls' dorm), 'Aunty Janet, how can we play on the swings and see-saws with all this junk lying about?' Even in the dim moonlight we could see that our lovely playground was in a mess. Planks of wood, bags of cement, piles of bricks—the lot.

'S-sh, girls,' whispered Aunty Janet. I don't know why. Even though it was midnight, there was no one in bed to waken!

'In the morning,' she said, 'I'll tell you everything.'

I hoped I was going to *like* Aunty Janet. Imagine 'in the morning'! I was bursting with curiosity right *then*. I was pretty sure that Aunty *Eva* would have told us. I had a very unworthy thought in my frustration—I was almost sorry I had managed *not* to be sick over her feet when I stumbled out of the taxi!

Morning came quickly, after all. When we woke up, bright sunlight was flooding the dorm, even though the curtains were still drawn. Suddenly I was wide awake, in spite of the fact that I'd only had a few hours sleep. It was morning, we were back at Chefoo and Aunty Janet had something to tell us!

I leapt out of bed, which was a big mistake. I'd completely forgotten that this was the middle-sized-girls' dorm and I no longer slept on a low bed near the floor. In fact, I had been given the top tier of a bunk bed!

The thump with which I hit the floor resulted in three things:

1 Everybody else woke up.
2 Abigail Fischer started to giggle. (She had moved up a dorm too, and cruel fate had put her in the bunk under me.)
3 Cruel Fate (i.e. Aunty Janet) tore in, in a mild sort of madness.

The first day had begun!

When I had picked myself off the floor, still all in one piece, I made for the window and wrenched back the curtains. Yes! It was true, and all the more obvious in the bright daylight. The playground was covered in building materials. I also became aware that a certain amount of banging and hammering was going on not far away.

A tousled-headed bunch of girls surrounded Aunty Janet as she perched on the toy-locker. Only about half of us were back so far. The Singapore party would be due at lunch time.

That was my second mistake!—all inside five minutes, too! For Aunty Janet dropped quite a bombshell.

'The rest of the Chefoo kids aren't coming back—not for another week,' she began.

'Not for another week? Extra holiday? Whatever for?' called Abigail Fischer. Immediately she had cottoned on to something she thought was unfair.

'*I*'ve had a long enough holiday,' I said, just to show her up.

'S-sh,' said Aunty Janet. It was her favourite word. 'Girls, you must cooperate.'

'Aunty Janet, do go on,' begged Stella, tugging at her sleeve.

And then Aunty Janet told us all about that landslide. It had rained in the Camerons, she said, for eleven days without stopping once! No wonder the land had started to slide. All over the highlands, mountain sides had come hurtling down, causing dreadful damage and loss of life, and blocking the mountain road.

'I never noticed any slides on the road last night,' announced Fish.

'How could you, in the dark?' I asked sweetly.

The sunlight was hot on our pyjama-ed backs. It was hard to imagine a morning, only a few weeks ago, when the sky was grey and the merciless rain poured down on a crumbling Chefoo.

It was a surprised group who gathered for morning prayers that first Monday of term. The assembly hall was still half empty. *We* (the Thai party) were back only because our travel tickets had already been bought and our visas seen to before the accident. It was easy to see Mr Melville's table that day—not too many heads in Levels 1 and 2 to crane round! A huge jug and some piles of building stuff decorated the top of the table.

Into the story of the wise and foolish men he plunged— almost literally! The foolish man's site for his Lego house was a flat pile of sandy soil. A large even stone held up the wise man's quarters. The storm came next. That was when the jug came into action—it contained the rain! The Head poured a great deluge on both the houses. You can guess what happened! The sandy soil slipped away—right off the table, in fact, on to Aunty Anna's clean polished floor!

And then work for the week started—lessons which included us making our own landslides! *Everything* was about landslides! Sloshing about in the mud was the best school lesson I ever had in my life! As we discovered how wet the soil must be before it will slip down an incline, I had the chance to squirt a squishy lump of semi-liquid soil at Fish. It landed right on target too—on her fat cheek—and she never saw where it came from! That was Maths and Science.

Have you ever played with mud and felt it s-s-slip and s-s-slide? I loved the gooey mess so much that I was sorry to have to go into the classroom after our experiments. However, we wrote about it. Here's our poem:

This word is LANDSLIDE which brought us dismay.

L is for LANDSLIDE which knocked down a wall,
A for AUNT ANNA who found it all.
N is for NOTEBOOKS, floating out the door,
D is for DESKS upside down on the floor.
S is for SWEEPING away all the flood,
L's for LAU HUAT who removed all the mud.
I is for INK, floating out with the tide,
D's for safe DORM above, where we reside.
E is for EVERYTHING which happened that day,
This word is LANDSLIDE which brought us dismay.

By Level 3

Do you like it? I made up line 4.

For Art that week I produced an effort which showed the Chinese builder's truck, driving off with a load of mud. The mud in my picture was real! I helped myself to some left-over landslide soil, damped it and stuck it on to the lorry with sticky tape! The mountain behind looked fairly real too. I stuck green jungle ferns on to it. I even dressed Lau Huat in a yellow cloth shirt.

Our class composed a song too. It featured Mr Melville, sweeping out the muddy tide in his bare feet! We sang it to him at the little programme we all gave at the end of the week in the assembly hall. Every class had to say what they had discovered from their experiments and what they had learnt. A great hoot of laughter went up when Level 6 said that their study had gone wrong somewhere—somehow their land had slipped down their angled planks better when it was *dry*! Level 5 did a little play about Aunty Anna discovering the slide, only they had Mr M dashing down to the scene actually in his pyjamas! They called it DISASTER.

Looking back, I don't really think it was a disaster. If the main pillar, holding up the dorm above, had been hit—well, yes. Or, if we'd been *in* the classroom when the slide happened, yes. But we were all safe at home and though one wall came down, it could have been much worse.

Unfortunately, the next Monday dawned eventually. All the school was back. Morning prayers that day was a Praise service. Mr M thanked God that we were all safe and that everything was now okay, due to the fact that a Christian engineer 'just happened' to be up in the mountains when we needed him! The Head asked God to keep us safe in the wet season every year, because there'd always be that danger in the Camerons. And God has. That angel I told you about seems to work overtime!

5

A PARTY AND A PUZZLE

'He's been gone six hours!' whispered the voice.

'Six hours? Oh, I'm afraid he *is* lost,' came back a soft answer.

'What on earth can we do?' the first voice asked.

'I think . . .' began the other, but I missed the rest, for the legs carrying the voices slowly walked away from the honeycombed wall behind which I was standing.

My heart was hammering and my mouth felt dry. *Who* was lost? Could it be Frisky—the big black school Labrador? Or Louby Lou, Chefoo's little tabby cat?

I hadn't meant to eavesdrop. Behind the honeycombed wall the stairs led up to our dorm. I was just on my way down, dressed up as Captain Scott, when I became aware of the whispering voices.

Until that moment my thoughts had been full of our class party. Today was the day. Class Party days took place once a term. They were to make up for the birthday parties we missed through not being at home. When our birthdays came we had juice, cake and presents with our class members gathered round us after school. I had been nine in September and had enjoyed it all very much—especially the parcel from Mum which turned out to be roller skates. Roller-skating on the netball court was the new *in* thing at Chefoo.

But today was even more special than *real* birthday-day! At last it was Class Party day and now—something or somebody was lost.

Lifting my heavy boots, I clumped back up the stairs.

'Stella,' I called, bursting in on our group who were all in the various stages of dressing up, ready for the big do.

Ann Boleyn, one of Henry VIII's ill-fated wives, daintily danced across the room.

'Stella MacAlpine, is that really you under that bonnet? Well, come out here,' I dropped my voice. 'I know a secret.'

Stella and I stood on the balcony outside the door. I whispered what I'd heard.

'Oh Toots, you shouldn't have listened!' scolded Stella. Stella, by the way, is sometimes too good to be true.

'I couldn't help it!' I breathed earnestly. 'I was just going down the stairs.'

'Who were the two you heard?' asked Stella.

'There you are!' I said triumphantly. 'You're just as curious as I am! One was Miss Fletcher, for sure, but I couldn't see her. I don't know who the other was.'

'Well, we'd better forget it,' advised Stella. 'It's only five minutes to go until party time.'

At last we tripped down the staircase with a throng of other famous characters from British history. It was only ten minutes since I'd been down before, when all was so quiet, and yet now it seemed as if the whole school had assembled to see us arrive! Word had got round that some celebrities were visiting Chefoo that day, and everyone wanted to see them! The Head even arrived with his camera, and we had to line up against the wall and grin self-consciously. After that Miss Fletcher and Aunty Janet arrived dressed up as Queen Elizabeth I and Gladys Aylward, so the Head had to start and take pictures all over again. No one had guessed our teacher and dorm aunty were dressing up too!

. . . we had to line up, against the wall and grin self-consciously.

That means, I said to myself, that *Queen Elizabeth I* must have been standing right by that wall in her big full gown when I heard that secret.

Who could have been lost? Was he, she or it *still* lost?

I pushed the mystery out of my mind and joined the others as they shoved into the assembly hall in their flashy clothes.

'Great ladies and gentlemen often went to balls and danced together,' announced our teacher—I mean, Queen Elizabeth I. 'We will do our Swedish Clap Dance. Take a partner, everyone.' Miss Fletcher arranged the huge folds of her dress around her as she seated herself at the piano.

Florence Nightingale stepped out with Sir Walter Raleigh. Over in the corner, Lord Nelson grabbed Elizabeth Fry by the waist and performed some very awkward steps.

I made out Fish's plump form under the garb of Mary Queen of Scots. The *real* Queen would have turned in her grave, if she'd seen her. Philip Tate, dressed up as Oliver Cromwell, unwillingly led her into the circle.

It was time I found a partner myself. I heaved my coil of rope higher on my shoulder, lifted my pick-axe and found Stella. We had a good giggle together.

After the dance, Miss Fletcher and Aunty Janet judged our costumes. I was disappointed not to get a prize, for at least I'd been original—I was the only girl who had dressed up as a man. However, they decided that Paul Carter deserved first prize. I must admit, he did look rather grand as Julius Caesar. I think it was the helmet bit that won for him. William the Conqueror came second and Lady Jane Grey third.

Paul Carter was looking extra pleased with himself—smug, you could say. You see, his *mother* was at the party. Actually, his father was meant to be there too but hadn't been able to make it. Sometimes mums and dads came to the Cameron Highlands for their holidays so that they could see their children in the middle of term. It's a good climate too, of course, for at 5,000 feet up you don't feel the tropical heat of the plains. Mrs Carter sat clutching her handbag and smiling at Paul.

It was a good thing actually to get all the judging done at the beginning for, as the party wore on, our costumes wore off! All sorts of bits and pieces littered the sides of the hall.

The grub was great! We'd chosen it ourselves! I had written out the list of items we'd voted for in my weekly letter to Mum. It looked like this:

MENU
for
LEVEL IV CLASS PARTY

Main course: Satay and Peanut Sauce
Sweet course: Chocolate Chip Cookies
              White meringues with pink icing
              Angel Cake

Special afters: Toffee Apples

Drinks: Choice of bottled drinks from Tanah Rata.

As the Satay arrived, I saw Fish rub her stomach. Then the new boy who was just back from a year's leave, made us all roar with laughter.

'I voted for Satay,' he said, 'but I hadn't a clue what it was!'

'Well, as you can see, it's little pieces of meat on a skewer, sort of barbecued,' pointed out Mrs Carter, who was a missionary further south in Malaysia. 'It's a special Malay dish.'

We decided to keep our toffee apples until the end of the party. The Head was going to show us some funny films and as we goggled we were going to munch in the dark.

Aunty Janet, I mean Gladys Aylward, had great ideas for games. I nearly had a fit when I saw the picture I drew, because we had an art lesson in the dark. After that we played 'Aunt Miranda went to Paris and she bought a fan'. Do you know it? If you want to play it, you'd better practise being cooperated! No, that doesn't sound right—I think it's 'coordinated'. That's the new word our party taught me. I already knew 'cooperate'. That's what we have to do in the dorm. Aunty Janet asks us to, at least once a day.

Then Queen Liz stood up. 'I see we have Lord Nelson here,' she said. 'Well, Lord Nelson, we need you here for this game, called "Nelson's Eye".'

Three people were chosen to go outside the room. I was one. We stood giggling and expectant on the other side of the door, wondering what was going on. Whispers were coming from inside, and muffled laughter.

The door opened.

'Right, Captain Scott,' called Miss Fletcher, 'in you come.'

I didn't *want* to be first, but I'd no option. I walked in, feeling a bit trembly and wondering what they were going to do to me.

I soon found out. It was short and felt quite weird. First I was blindfolded. Miss Fletcher took my elbow (at least, I think it was she).

'Captain Scott,' she said. 'We have here today the noted sea captain, Lord Nelson. You've heard of him? Do come and meet him. Yes, this is definitely Lord Nelson. Do you want me to prove it?'

I nodded, wishing that the nodding would knock the scarf from my eyes. I felt sure some sort of trick was coming!

'Here,' said Miss Fletcher, taking my hand, 'feel his good arm.'

I could feel Jimmy Martin's bony elbow under the Lord Nelson jacket.

'Now,' went on Miss Fletcher, 'feel his bad arm.'

Somehow they presented me with an empty sleeve, and I realized that of course old Nelson had lost an arm.

'Feel Nelson's good leg', said Miss Fletcher.

It went all against the grain to be feeling Jimmy Martin's baggy trousers, but I had to.

'And his *bad* leg,' continued Miss Fletcher.

Something hard hit against the palm of my hand. I found out afterwards that it was the broom handle, and wondered vaguely if it was true that Nelson had lost a leg at Trafalgar. I had thought the other thing missing had been his eye.

Anyway, we were coming to that.

'Feel Nelson's good eye,' instructed Miss Fletcher, guiding my hand down Jimmy Martin's face.

'And now,' she rushed on, all at once, 'his bad eye.'

Before I had time to think, my forefinger struck something squishy and gooey.

'Ugh!' I yelled.

The class roared. They had obviously been waiting for that moment and, as their merriment rang out, visions of a bloody, gory eye went through my mind.

'Ugh!' I yelled again, and with my unsmeared hand tore off the blindfold.

A bright red tomato was the first thing I saw, and stuck to my forefinger was half of its over-ripe inside.

I tried to laugh too, and as the others were hauled in for their turns of finding Nelson's eye, I *really* laughed and saw the funny side of it. For the rest of the evening, Captain Scott had tomato juice down his shirt front. It

was the nearest thing to wipe my gory finger on!
And so the fun went on.

It's a queer sensation feeling sad when you're watching funny films! But that's what happened to me. You see, when the Head arrived with his projector, it was the beginning of the end, and I'd never been to such a good class party. True, the last one we'd had was meant to be my best. It was a GMTP—that stands for Ghost Mining Town Party. We'd panned for silver in the stream that day, and dug gold out of the Head's flowerbeds! We'd had shows at the Silver Palace and had sung 'Oh my darling Clementine'. That sure was a good party, but so was this. I wish parties would never come to an end. I was so *sorry* it was nearly over, that I nearly forgot to laugh at Charlie Chaplin.

The second film had just been looped into the projector when we were all quite startled to hear running footsteps. The assembly hall door was pushed open and slammed shut again immediately. Everyone looked round, Pluto and Mickey Mouse forgotten.

'Mr Melville,' panted a voice, which I recognized as belonging to Aunty Mary, the school nurse. 'Mr Melville—an urgent telephone call! Can you come at once?'

The Head switched off the projector. The room was suddenly very dark. He dashed to the door, tripping over the flex as he did so.

'Mrs Carter,' he called through the blackness, 'I think you should come with me.'

Was that the end of the show? I suddenly realized I *loved* cartoons after all—especially if you've a toffee apple to munch.

Queen Liz groped her way to the light switch.

'We'll have a guessing game,' she said, 'while we wait for the Head to come back.'

The only thing I wanted to guess was why he'd gone. Strange—taking Paul's mother with him. Pity Mr Carter couldn't come to the party—especially when Paul had won a prize as old Julius Caesar.

I took a bite of my toffee apple.

Just then the door opened and the Head breezed in again. The lights were still on. I saw him smile at Aunty Janet and Miss Fletcher. He gave them a 'thumbs up' signal.

Mrs Carter wasn't with him.

The film show continued without interruption. I laughed in all the right places but my mind wasn't really on Laurel and Hardy. It wasn't even on my juicy toffee apple. Lost! The word kept going round in my head. Who was lost? Was that telephone call anything to do with it?

Party Day came to an end. *Next* Friday, Level 2, including Patrick, would have their big day. They were to have a Cowboys and Indians Party and were going to put up a tepee. The previous week the top class had had a Cookout. Every class thought their party was best!

The party was over, but the mystery wasn't. That night I snuggled under the covers of my top-tier bunk. I should have been tired after all the fun, but I wasn't. A full moon had risen over the jungle-clad hills and was bathing our dorm in its pale light. I could hear Stella's light breathing in the next top bunk. Obviously she was asleep already. Fish was moving restlessly down below, making the whole bunk shake.

Lost! I wished I knew who was lost.

I settled myself to say a few whispered prayers, lying down with my eyes wide open.

'Thank you for class parties,' I began. 'Thank you that Christian people at home give money for us to have good grub at parties. Thank you that someone sent Mr Melville money to buy funny films. . . .' My eyes were beginning to close. Hurriedly I tacked on one more thought. 'Lord . . . whoever's lost . . . please look after them.'

One good thing about Class Parties is that Saturdays come next. The sun was streaming into our dorm when I woke up—rather later than usual.

And what did I think about first? Right! That lost thing! As soon as I could, I checked up on Louby Lou and Frisky. Louby was asleep on the library cushions and Frisky was digging for a hidden bone down by the stream. I could find no answer to the puzzle of the whispered conversation.

Nearly all the kids from the top dorms were zooming round on their skates on the netball court. I joined them. At first I paid no attention to the little buzzing group around Paul Carter. Then snatches of conversation began to come my way.

'Have you heard?'

'Bad fright . . .'

'Six hours in the jungle!'

'Glad it wasn't my dad.'

Quick as a shot I put two and two together. Mr Carter!

I zipped over to the group around Paul. It had grown now but I could hear everything he was saying. In fact, I skated beside him for the rest of the morning until I'd heard every detail.

On Party Day, Paul's father had decided to climb Erau—that's our highest mountain. It's unusual for climbers to go up these mountains alone—they are covered in jungle and you have to make your way up by a steep tangled trail. But Mr Carter was an experienced climber. It was a heavenly day, and he wanted a bit of exercise.

Just where he lost the path he never knew, but it was true that he was up there, in the jungle, all by himself and could not get down. It's an extremely dangerous thing to be lost in the jungle—what with tigers and snakes and so on.

At supper time, just when we were digging into Satay and peanut sauce, three of the men from the holiday bungalow set off to look for him before darkness fell.

It's a good thing they got him. Not everyone has been found who gets lost up there. But these men were able to locate Mr Carter by calling. By that time he was badly scared and had to be treated for shock. So when the telephone call came, Mrs Carter had gone right away—back to the holiday bungalow to look after him.

And Paul didn't know a thing about it till the next day. After that he just about told everybody of the adventures of *his* dad. No wonder! But I'm glad it wasn't mine.

I never think of parties now without remembering Paul's father. Paul says God kept his dad safe. The more I think about it, the more I'm inclined to agree. Or perhaps it was that angel, busy again.

6

THE MYSTERY OF THE MISSING FRANC

It was that same year that our class became involved in the Mystery of the Missing Franc.

Maths lessons were the whole cause of the trouble— they always are as far as I'm concerned. Maths is just my *hatredest* subject. Anyway, Miss Fletcher was trying to teach us to add money.

Adding money can be a bit complicated anywhere, but at Chefoo it was a real headache. Do you know the word 'international'? International is what we are. That means that in Chefoo there are children from all over the world.

Paul Carter, for instance, is from South Africa. Jimmy Martin, the bony one, is a New Zealander. Five of us are American citizens, Fish and Rosemary are both Australians, and the rest of us, including me, are British. Oh no—I nearly forgot, we've got a Swiss girl too. In fact, several of the classes have children from the Continent of Europe—all being educated in English.

Does that give you a clue as to how complicated it is to add money in our class—I mean, which money do you add? The only money most of us knew anything about was Malay dollars and cents. Miss Fletcher said that wasn't enough to know, because we had to be able to do money sums in our home countries when we left Chefoo. So she set up a classroom shop.

This was no ordinary shop, I can tell you. It was called Chefoo Chemist Shop, and it operated in four currencies. Every tin of talc, every bottle of perfume, each deodorant —was priced *four* times! Behind the 'counter' on the notice board was a complete list which read like this:

CHEFOO CHEMIST SHOP

PRICES

Item	USA	Australia	UK	Malaysia
Perfume	$2.10	$1.75	£0.87	$4.70
Talc	$1.50	$1.18	£0.59	$2.76
Hand cream	$1.20	$0.85	£0.47½	$2.50
Face cream	$2.05	$1.66	£0.83	$4.32
Lipstick	$1.55	$1.30	£0.65	$3.00
Hairspray	$0.95	$0.75	£0.37½	$1.95
Nail varnish	$1.10	$0.90	£0.45	$2.45
Deodorant	$0.85	$0.70	£0.35	$1.65
Aftershave	$1.80	$1.55	£0.77	$4.05
Hair cream	$1.05	$0.87	£0.43½	$2.40

If you could get past the smell that surrounded the counter, you had to pick up assignment cards which consisted of all sorts of complicated shop bills. The ones I hated most were where you had to find the change. That was when I felt sorry I was British. We were the only nation that thought of the half-penny. I can tell you I don't think much of the council who decided on half-pennies for the British system. Miss Fletcher said not to complain, because it was much more complicated when she was a little girl, with all sorts of weird numbers like 240 pence in a pound and 12 pennies in a shilling.

Anyway, since those days Britain had 'gone decimal' like the rest of the world. We had learnt decimals but there were no fractions in any decimal sums that I ever did. In fact, the teacher said you never mix the two. Well, she was wrong, because the British did, and that's how you get a daft price like £0.37½ for a can of hairspray.

I'll have to admit, though, that apart from the half-pennies the classroom shop was quite good fun. You had to go and 'buy' at it, and hand over *real* money for all your jars and bottles. All I can say is, the staff must use a powerful amount of smelling things if a whole table of empty containers could be found just when we were ready to have a shop.

Well, one day when we were sitting around the floor in groups, practising counting out money from our own country, Colette the Swiss girl said to Miss Fletcher that she had a French franc and could she go to the dorm to get it?

Miss Fletcher was all delighted to display it, and we had a little lecture on the value of francs and centimes to tie in with our French lessons.

The franc was set on top of the bookcase along with the four boxes of money from the other countries. After a few days, the novelty of having it had worn off, and we got used to seeing it there.

Just when it disappeared, none of us knew. At least none of us seemed to know, but about a week later, Colette, who is rather emotional, and also quite blunt, screamed out in the middle of our calculations, 'It's gone! My franc's gone! Who took it?'

All of a sudden there was a great silence—quite a

Miss Fletcher had all her boxes of money carefully counted, and was keeping a watchful eye on them!

contrast to the jingling of coins that had filled the room just a second before. Everyone looked—first at Colette, next at the empty spot on the bookcase, and then at Miss Fletcher to see what she would do.

Miss Fletcher did not turn a hair. Mildly she said, 'Colette dear, it's probably slipped down behind the bookcase.'

Colette, being the emotional type she was, insisted on pulling out the bookcase there and then. This was quite a job, for all the dictionaries, histories, spelling books and so on had to be lifted off the shelves before anyone could get the thing moved.

However, after all this effort, the French franc was nowhere to be seen. It wasn't among the books either, or along the louvered window-frame, or behind the picture on the wall, or anywhere else any of us looked. We were *all* looking, of course, as solving this little mystery was more fun than the maths lesson.

'I told you someone took it,' wailed Colette.

'Sit down, everybody,' said Miss Fletcher, loudly and sternly. 'Really, what a to-do! Colette, if anyone wanted money I would expect them to help themselves from the Malaysian box. What good would a French franc be to anyone?'

Miss Fletcher had all her boxes of money carefully counted, and was keeping a watchful eye on them.

But Colette wailed all the louder. 'I *know* someone took it,' she exclaimed, and then, with a sinister note in her voice, 'someone who added it to her coin collection.'

You could have heard a franc drop—only there was no franc.

And then it dawned on me *who* had taken that franc. It was Abigail Fischer. I just *knew* it was, and now we had the absolute proof. Everyone knew she had a coin collection. Everyone knew it was her one great hobby— besides annoying other law-abiding people.

The mean creature, I thought to myself. It was on the tip of my tongue to say that *Fish* had a coin collection when Miss Fletcher breathed, her voice dangerously quiet, 'I said, "Sit down, all of you". Get on with your counting. I don't want to hear one more word about coin collections. Colette, we'll go into the matter later.'

Colette gave an emotional sniff, and with a bad grace joined the Malaysian money-counting group again.

But, of course, the affair of the disappearing franc didn't end there. All of us had now got it into our heads that someone had added a French franc to a coin collection. It seemed a reasonable suggestion, as there was nothing else to do with a French franc. I mean, the cleaning girls wouldn't want it, nor the workmen, nor anyone else we could think of.

Classroom life had to go on, of course. The next lesson was Creative Writing. Fortunately Hank Barrows broke the smouldering tension by calling out loudly, 'Miss Fletcher, how do you spell "plough"? I'm an American.' Spelling caused quite a bit of difficulty in our classroom, too, because we were an international group; but actually it meant you could get marks in the Friday test for a variety of answers, which suited me nicely.

After school, we girls always dashed up to our dorm to pour the problems of the classroom day into Aunty Janet's ears. Every day at half past three we changed our school clothes for shorts and play shirts. I struggled into my Méo costume. Aunty Janet was giving out a sweet each, and we were vying with each other for her attention.

'Aunty Janet, my zip's stuck!'

'Aunty Janet, will you tie back my hair again? It's sort of come undone since this morning.'

'Aunty Janet, I've cut my leg.'

'Aunty Janet, I can add American money as well as British.'

That did it. My thoughts were so full of that classroom mystery that, without thinking twice, I joined in the general uproar and yelled, 'Aunty Janet, did you hear about Abigail Fischer?'

'No, what about Gail?' asked Aunty Janet.

And without pausing I rushed on, 'She stole Colette's French franc for her coin collection.'

For the second time that day a sudden hush descended on our group. In that instant, I knew I had said the wrong thing.

The silence lengthened. In my mind I could hear my own voice shrilly announcing 'Abigail Fischer stole . . .

Abigail Fischer stole . . .' My face began to colour slowly until the very tips of my ears were bright crimson.

'I m . . . m . . . mean', I stammered, 'we *think* she stole . . .' What was I saying? I seemed to be making matters worse. Even Stella was looking at me wonderingly.

Just then Fish came bounding into the room. I hated the fat sight of her. Now she'd got me into a whole frying-pan-full of bother. Aunty Janet obviously didn't appreciate my conclusions about her character.

Quickly Aunty Janet broke the silence and changed the subject. 'Ah, there you are, Gail dear. Would you like your candy now?' And then, 'Teresa, hurry with changing, and stay for a moment. I'd like a word with you.'

Everyone else trooped out, trooped out with their roller skates to have fun on the netball court. The sunlight was pouring through our big dorm windows, but I felt cold and grey. All the fun had gone out of the day. Whatever had made me say that about Fish? I could see now, only five minutes later, that I had no proof at all that she took the franc; but I had so coddled the accusing thought all day in the classroom that I'd convinced myself that she had. Now I saw that I had manufactured the whole thing. I was always hopeless at maths. This was putting two and two together and making three!

Fish now sauntered out of the dorm too, noisily sucking a brandy ball. I saw where she'd left her school things strewn over the bed, and her sandals just where she'd stepped out of them. But Aunty Janet didn't even call her back to put them straight. She just kept on looking at me.

Then she sat down on Jill Peter's bed. 'Now, Teresa, what *is* all this?'

I stood there, curling up my toes, and remaining stubbornly silent.

'About a franc, Colette's franc,' prompted Aunty Janet.

'It disappeared,' I said gruffly, 'from the classroom bookcase.'

'I see. Did Gail take it?'

'I don't know,' I mumbled.

'But that's what you said, isn't it?'

Aunty Janet lifted Jill's Bible from the top of her locker.

'Listen to what it says in St Matthew, dear. "Judge not and . . ." '

I closed my ears. I didn't want to hear about St Matthew or any other saint for that matter. And I didn't even want to hear what Aunty Janet said.

'Do you hear that, dear?' asked Aunty Janet.

I nodded, but it was really a white lie; I had missed the little sermon that she'd tagged on to the text.

Christians and Bibles, I thought. I'm tired trying to live up to them. I hate Abigail Fischer, so I might as well give up trying to be a Christian.

Aunty Janet was continuing, '. . . and you *are* going to be a Christian, aren't you, dear?'

'No,' I snapped, 'I'm going to be a woman journalist.'

My mother would have been shocked. I suddenly could stand it no longer. Anything but being preached at. I ran over to my own bunk, fumbled my way up the ladder and flung myself down on the bed cover, sobbing and punching the pillow at the same time, in my frustration.

Half an hour later I raised my head and looked round. The bright sunlight still flooded the room—the *empty* room. Aunty Janet had left me to it.

I dabbed at my red eyes with the apron of my Méo costume. I raised my head and stared out of the window at the happy group on the netball court. Stella was tugging Abigail Fischer round on her roller skates. Stella and Fish! A few more tears of self-pity slipped down my hot cheeks. I lowered my gaze.

And then I saw it! There, glinting in the sunlight, shining on the window-sill, was a piece of money!

I blinked, rubbed my eyes and stared again. Yes, it was a coin. The sill was lower than my top-tier bunk so I reached down behind my bed and groped for the shining silver circle.

The franc!

I grasped it in my hot hand and simply stared at it. *Liberté. Egalité. Fraternité.* it said. *1960.*

At that very moment Colette walked into our dorm. She had decided to bring back her roller skates and get her jacks instead. I'd been so absorbed in what I had discovered that I hadn't heard her diving up the stairs.

She found me perched on the top-tier bunk staring at her French franc. I didn't even have time to hide it away.

'So *Gail* stole my French franc, did she?' she sneered.

Before I could gather my wits, she'd pounced on me and grabbed her franc.

I don't think I have ever wanted my mother so much in my life.

Instead, in walked Aunty Janet.

My heart was hammering. My face and my eyes were redder than ever. 'Aunty Janet,' I began, but Colette beat me to it.

'*She* had it. *She* had it all the time,' said Colette, pointing an accusing finger at me.

You know, I'd always liked Colette with her pretty foreign accent, even if she was a bit emotional. But now I wasn't so sure. In fact, I decided I would shout her down.

'That French franc has just appeared on my window-sill, Colette Dubois—if you want to know,' I snapped.

'Well, I am *so* glad it has turned up,' Aunty Janet interrupted hurriedly, with a note of relief in her voice. 'Colette dear, you may run along now. I'll try to sort the mystery out.'

You know, Aunty Janet was really a dear. I explained the whole thing to her, and she said of *course* she knew I hadn't taken it. She said that her guess was that the cleaning girl had swept it from the floor and set it on the window-sill for safety.

It sounded likely to me too, but how did the franc get from the bookcase in the classroom below, to the floor of the dorm above?

Anyway, the horrible afternoon was over. Our dorm was trooping up from the netball court to wash for supper. I joined them in an unnoticeable way. The franc had turned up. Everyone was talking about it. But its appearance was as mysterious as its disappearance. However, no one seemed to know any more about it—not yet, anyway.

7

A QUARTER TO NINE IN THE MORNING

'God sees the little sparrow fall,
It meets His tender view.
If God so loves the little things,
I know He loves me too.'

'He loves me too, He loves me too,' I sang gaily, though not too musically. I waved my hymn book about and sang my loudest. It was really a hymn for the little ones, but although I was almost ten, I really liked it.

'If God so loves the little things, I know . . .' I stopped! Right bang in the middle of the line! So did a whole lot of others. A few dwindling voices sang weakly to the end of the chorus.

Through the assembly hall door had marched Louby Lou. And Louby Lou had a tiny wee kitten in her mouth! She walked sedately through the stage curtains and returned at the end of the hymn with another!

The moment the piano stopped, our normal well-behaved assembly broke into a buzz of conversation.

Louby Lou had been lost! At least, we *thought* she was lost. We'd come back to school at the beginning of a new school year and there was no cat! Now the mystery was solved!

Three kittens arrived in all—all in their mother's mouth. Louby Lou had found a cosy box for them full of old stage clothes, on a corner of the platform.

'Now,' came Mr Melville's voice, booming over the din, 'Now we'll start our new school year with prayer.'

Settling down, we listened. I bet God has never heard a school year opened with a prayer like that before! We prayed for Louby Lou and her kittens and thanked God that He took care of little things just as we'd been singing! Imagine being right in the middle of *that* hymn on *that* particular morning! Louby Lou had made it special! Morning prayers *or* assembly, whichever it was called, I liked it.

Skipping back to class in the sun, we vied with one another for our new teacher's attention.

Fish was shouting, 'Miss Deane, who is Louby Lou's husband?'

'Don't really know,' answered our teacher. 'Maybe she has several!'

'But I mean—who's the *father* cat?' persisted Fish.

'I think it's that big black tom from the village,' volunteered Jill Peters. 'You can tell 'cos all the kittens have some black in them.'

'What on earth has *that* got to do with it?' demanded Fish, who was in a questioning mood.

'Don't you know *any*thing?' I asked her. 'Cats have to mate—like all other animals.' I liked airing my knowledge.

'What's *mating*?' asked Colette. Perhaps she only knew the word in French.

'I'll leave that for Mrs Melville to explain when Growing

Up Club starts,' Miss Deane decided. 'Now let's get into the classroom and get organized.'

Miss Deane was very fond of being organized, I found out. Her desk was always tidy. So was the rest of the room. We even had a trailing plant on the art cupboard.

But Fish didn't want to be organized. The very first morning back at school should be somewhat *dis*organized, she thought.

'Wonder what Monday morning assemblies will be this term,' she called out, banging her desk lid as she slid into her seat.

''Member last term?' Paul Carter joined in.

'Witness Box,' announced bony Jimmy Martin, as if none of us knew.

Miss Deane looked up. 'Okay,' she said, 'why not write down on this page what your favourite Monday in Witness Box was? While you're doing that, I'll get organized and give out your new Level 5 textbooks.'

A few stifled groans rumbled through the room. Work! So early in the term! I looked daggers at Fish who'd started it all. But—remember, I was going to be a woman journalist and I didn't really mind writing about things.

Do you know, when we came to read out what we'd written, every single one of us had chosen the same assembly! It was the day Dr Lambeth had been in the Witness Box.

The Head put him there.

'Do you promise to tell the truth, the whole truth, and nothing but the truth?'

'I do,' answered Dr Lambeth.

'Are you a Christian?'

'Yes.'

'You are the judges,' said the Head to us. 'I will question him and you can decide if he's guilty.'

He sure was. There was enough evidence to convict a roomful of doctors.

1 He'd spent 40 years in South-east Asia as a missionary,
2 He'd been a doctor in China *and* Thailand.
3 He'd been in a Japanese prison camp.
4 He'd been separated from his family for years, so that he could preach the Gospel.
5 In his retirement he'd offered to come to Chefoo School to be our school doctor.

'Guilty!' we shouted out.

Dr Lambeth didn't seem a bit worried.

'I'll sing to you now,' he said, '—my favourite song.'

Dr Lambeth was an old man by that time, but he was musical. He opened his hymn book and sang, 'Living for Jesus a life that is true'.

I think I remember the song most. Oh yes—there was one other thing I understood for the first time that day. I got the point about the blood of Jesus saving someone.

Dr Lambeth, one day, had to get blood for a dying man. He asked a Chinese relative for some. The relative was very scared. He'd never heard before of giving a pint of blood. He though *he'd* be the next to pop off if he did! But Dr Lambeth persuaded him.

The next day the dying man was getting better.

'Oh, thank you for saving his life,' said the Chinese relative.

'I didn't,' explained Dr Lambeth. 'You did. You gave your blood. And,' he continued, 'I know *another* story of Someone giving His blood to save.' Then he told him about Jesus.

I read out to the class what I had written about Dr Lambeth.

'We're all going to miss him terribly, this term,' Miss Deane said. Dr Lambeth had gone back to the States as he couldn't get a Visit Pass to stay with us any longer. Now we had no school doctor.

It was unlikely, I thought, that Monday morning assemblies would be as good this term as last. That was before I knew we were going to meet Boo Hoo, Toto, Twigga and all the animals out of the Jungle Doctor stories! They were on the screen, and we heard them on tape as well.

Tuesday was Drama morning. It was really the story of Samuel, but we acted it as we went along. I'll never forget Philip Tate doing old Eli! Little Patrick was chosen to be Samuel. He looked cute in his red dressing gown, snuffing out imaginary candles. Fish was Peninnah. She came on to the stage in her maxi, holding several kids by the hand and chanting to Stella, 'Hannah has no children. Hannah has no children.' You know, we didn't practise this acting. We just did it as the Head told the story.

On Wednesdays we went back to the classroom quite hoarse! It was Song Singing Day. To learn a new song, we had to pretend we were in an orchestra. You could play a violin and sing the tune to 'E . . . E . . . E . . . E.' Or you could be a pianist and go 'Lah . . . Lah . . . Lah . . . Lah.' We twanged guitars, blew trumpets, waved tambourines, and clashed cymbals—the lot. Then, of course, we knew the tune and could sing the words.

On Friday mornings at assembly we saw about the lives of twentieth-century Christians on the overhead projector.

And sometimes on Fridays classes put on a programme to tell us all what they'd been learning.

I'd like to have left out what happened on Thursdays. You see—about the middle of that term, it made me think too much! I don't like having a guilty conscience. I had one then, and I had the greatest trouble getting rid of it.

Maybe you are wondering, 'What could Toots have been guilty about?' Of course you know that I hadn't stolen—not the French franc anyway. Yet, ever since that incident, I'd never said any prayers! I knew very well that I should have been saying prayers, and I knew I should never have blamed Fish for lifting the coin, but when it turned out that *I* got into trouble, I hated Fish worse than ever. She just made me so mad, I could see no point in pretending I was a Christian.

The only thing was—I hadn't really been pretending about it. I *was* a Christian. At home, up in our little Méo village, I had asked the Lord Jesus to take away my sins. My mum says He did. I also asked Him to help me live my life for Him.

It's all very well taking a decision like that when life's good and happy and you're home for the holidays. But the holidays don't last for ever and, back at school, there was Fish.

I didn't say anything to mum and dad about giving up being a Christian. I just kept quiet about it and let everything slip. Into the bargain, I disliked Abigail Fischer more than ever.

So I had a guilty conscience.

'Here is my own private Letter Box,' announced the Head, the first Thursday morning. He held up a bright red box with a white lid like a little cap on top. 'This will hang outside my office all week.'

I could see white writing on the front. It said 'Thursday Post Box'.

'Here is its mouth,' said the Head. 'Inside here you post your letters.'

Us?

'Yes,' said the Head. 'I want *you* to write to *me*. Have you a problem, or a question about the Bible? Is there something you can't find an answer to? Well, just pop your question in here, and on Thursday mornings I'll try to answer it.'

Up shot a hand. I might have known. It was Abigail Fischer's.

'Yes, Gail?'

'Have you to sign your name to the question?' demanded Fish.

'No. Not at all. Not if you don't want to,' replied Mr Melville.

I could hardly wait till the next Thursday to see if anyone had asked a question.

The Head opened the white lid and took out three folded pieces of paper. They looked very mysterious.

We held our breath in expectation.

'In Exodus chapter 34 verse 14 it says that God is jealous. I thought God was perfect,' read out the Head.

It took him three and a half minutes to explain it. I timed it on my new watch that I'd got in advance for my birthday.

'Mr Melville, how does God exist? Did He make Himself, or not?'

I forgot to time that one. I was listening for the answer.

'Last one for today,' announced the Head. 'If your name is in the Book of Life, if you do a wrong thing, will your name be blotted out?'

'Those were good questions,' said Mr Melville finally. 'Some more for next week!'

And then, of course, I got my idea. Why not put a question in the box myself? One about the problem of hating Fish!

I carefully camouflaged my writing.

For two weeks I thought about it. My birthday came and went before I could pluck up the courage to write the thing out. Then I carefully camouflaged my writing. In a backhand scrawl on a piece of white paper I wrote, 'Can you be a Christian and hate someone like mad?'

Even when I had written it out, I was scared to post it in case someone saw me. I carried it round for a whole day until it was quite crumpled up, but at last I saw my chance. The supper bell had gone and I was late. No one was in sight when I scampered down past the office. I delved into my pocket and got the note out. My heart was pounding as I slipped it into the box. No one saw me. Slightly flustered, I at last arrived in the dining room.

'Late again, Toots,' scolded Aunty Janet. 'I do wish you'd cooperate.' But it was worth the scolding!

Would next Thursday be the day my question would be picked out? I sat in assembly with my heart thudding loudly against my ribs.

'This first question is about hating,' announced the Head.

My heart hammered faster and I held my breath.

But it was pink paper the Head was reading from. 'Why does the Bible say that to love the Lord you must hate your father and mother?' Quite a teaser, I thought.

'And the second question is also about hating,' Mr Melville went on.

This would be it. I knew it. And it was.

'Can you be a Christian and hate someone like mad?'

Quite a few people giggled. *I* tried to look unconcerned. I was really listening as hard as I could.

'If anyone says "I love God" but keeps on hating his brother, he is a liar; for if he doesn't love his brother who is right there in front of him, how can he love God whom he has never seen? And God himself has said that one must love not only God, but his brother too,' read the Head from the Living Bible.

Well, at least Fish wasn't my brother. Maybe this verse wasn't for me. Underneath I wanted to go on with my hating. Right there in front of me was Fish, fatly sitting and sucking the ends of her hair.

'It isn't possible to love God unless you love the people you live with,' said Mr Melville.

'Yes, it *is*,' I said—into myself, of course. Didn't I love God and hate Fish?

'You only imagine you love God if that is so,' continued the Head. 'This verse means you must *prove* you love God by loving others.'

'That's impossible!' I said—again to myself. 'How can I possibly love someone that I don't even like?'

'The Bible says it is easy to love people who are good to you. Even sinners can do that. The test of real Christianity is to love . . . wait for it . . . your *enemies*.'

Hmmmm . . .

'Start off,' said the Head, 'by forgiving them. Then practise loving them—even if you don't feel like it.'

How on earth could I practise loving Fish?

I wondered if I could possibly have spoken my thoughts aloud, for Mr Melville was suddenly saying, 'Do something nice for your enemy today.'

'No!' I thought. 'I will *not* do something nice for Fish.'

With everyone else I stamped out of assembly. I was disgusted. The Christian life was miles too difficult for me.

I forgot about those miles as we launched into the metric system in the classroom. But, all the same, it seemed that the Head's words were written in my brain. They kept popping up when I didn't want to think about them. 'Do something nice for your enemy today.' I thought about Maths, English, French, Art—anything to forget the insistence of them. They were like drum beats hammering away at my conscience. I began to wish I'd never written the wretched question.

After school I played 'Capture the Flag' with the boys—I was in the mood for a rough game. That night I went to bed struggling to think of pleasant things, but the drum beat hammered me to sleep. My last waking thought was, 'Ha! The day's past. I got through it without doing anything nice for Fish.'

8

NO GOAL

Brian Kidd rose to score the goal which clinched the issue for Manchester United. The film squeaked to an end and the lights came on again in Dorm 4 accompanied by an avalanche of clapping.

'Sir, let's have it again!'

'Sir, let's see it backwards!'

'Sir, how about a Charlie Chaplin?'

'That's all for tonight, boys, I'm afraid,' Mr Melville said, when at last he could get a word in edgeways. 'Aunty Jenny would have had you all settled by now if she was on duty. Come on now, into bunks!' (Aunty Jenny had gone down with a virus.)

'Sir, I wish *I* could play in a match like that!' It was Patrick speaking. The European Cup Final film had taken his fancy in a far greater way than Charlie Chaplin or Laurel and Hardy.

The Head's reply was quick and had a devastating effect on my young brother. 'You mightn't have long to wait, my boy! Listen hard at assembly tomorrow morning!'

Getting to sleep was a tough job after news like that! Did the Head mean ... ? Could he, Patrick Thrower, only eight and a half years old, possibly be chosen for the School Team? Patrick was turning out to be a star performer, but most of the Chefoo Chieftains were ten or eleven years old.

Having a brother growing up at Chefoo made me realize that life didn't revolve solely around us girls. It opened my eyes to the fact that every Wednesday the boys, dressed in red shirts and white shorts, hurtled down the drive in the van after school. Two hours later they'd be back, rowdily hooting and yelling of victory.

Every Monday, too, they monopolized the playing field, rain or shine, as they practised for Wednesdays. I remember one particular day when the sky was grey and the rain teeming down, and they played on the field in their bathing trunks and bare feet, gaily kicking a ball through the great puddles. Watching from our balcony, it seemed to me that soccer in the rain was more fun than soccer in the sun. For the first time, I *almost* envied Patrick being a boy!

Wednesdays, therefore, were always more exciting for the boys. All the same, there was one thing I loved, and that was when the van load of them returned after the supper bell had rung. In the comparative quietness of the dining hall, we'd hear Mr M's tooting on the horn as he rounded the bend in the drive. The tooting didn't stop. It got louder and louder, and as the van spilled its occupants we'd hear

'2 – 4 – 6 – 8 –
Whom do we appreciate?
C – H – E – F – O – O.'

and we'd know that red arms would be waving, shirts flying, and a general hullaballoo would be going on out there.

After that there would be dead silence and we'd wait for it! The team would creep round under the dining-room windows and bob-up, all at once, absolutely *yelling* the score at us! It sort of disturbed the aimed-for peace in the dining room, where Aunty Janet liked us to cooperate and behave like ladies. We girls never actually *said*, 'congratulations', but wow, we were jolly proud all the same!

And now Patrick had a chance of being picked for the Chieftains! No wonder he could hardly sleep!

His dream came true, for sure enough his name was read out at assembly next morning. It was song singing day and I was hoarse as usual, but I felt like cheering.

'Patrick Thrower', the Head said, 'is having his big chance today! Although the yougest boy in the team, he will play goalie for Chefoo.'

And later I saw it down in black and white myself where it was pinned to the Notice Board.

Wednesday, March 21st

CHEFOO CHIETFAINS *v.* TENGKU ABDUL RAHMAN SCHOOL
FIRST XI

Time . . . 4 p.m.
Place . . . Army Camp, Slim Lines

TEAM
Patrick Thrower
Paul Carter   Jimmy Martin   Hank Barrows   Tim Peters
Bernard Fletcher   John King
Justyn Melville   Philip Tate   Kevin Charles   Tim White

Mr M was in charge of the team himself, and at quarter to four he had them all rounded up to go. At a fair pace the Volkswagen swept round the drive, followed by our other van, full of spectators. Today, for the first time, I was going too.

Down the winding roads we sped. At one stage we nearly hit the team for six as Mr M suddenly rammed on his brakes. He had to. Swerving out of a side road came a huge lorry-load of durians.

Ugh! We scrambled for our hankies and covered up our noses. Still the foul odour seeped through. *Who* could like the smell of durian? Well, the Chinese could—it was their favourite fruit—but to us it smelt like a mixture of drains and perspiration!

The pong died down at last and we arrived at the playing field. I couldn't even try to describe the match—I don't know enough about it—but one thing will stand out in my memory for years to come. It was a thing which sent the Chefoo Chieftains home in silence, and for the first time no heads bobbed up at the dining room window to yell the score. Even before they saw Mr M carrying a white-faced Patrick up the stairs, Stella said, she knew something was wrong.

Patrick was playing brilliantly—even I could see that. He needed to, for Blue Socks was on the opposing team. He was a little Malay boy, quick as the wind and forever trying to score a goal for his team. The Malays are small for their age, but skilful.

'*Lari, lari, lari*,' yelled the supporters of the Malay team. (*Lari* means Run.) They were shouting at Blue Socks. He was tearing up the side and making right for Patrick's territory once again.

Courageously Patrick flung himself at the feet of the advancing forward. Somehow his arm just got between

Blue Socks and the ball. There was a sickening thud as Blue Socks' right toe collided with Patrick's elbow.

That was the end of the match.

Patrick, looking like a ghost, was laid on Mr M's raincoat at the side of the field. Somehow he had to be got into the van. He was obviously very sick and weak from pain. I felt a dizzy pins-and-needles sensation creep over me too. I couldn't speak one word in the van on the way back to Chefoo, even when Fish said not to worry, he'd be all right. That only increased my sense of shock. I thought, 'That's all very well for you—*your* brother's alive and well.'

I couldn't speak one word in the van on the way back to Chefoo.

I suppose if you play sports, run about and climb, you take risks. By the law of averages, you *ought* to have an accident now and then. Only we'd never had an accident at soccer before, not since I'd been there—so why did it have to happen to my brother? And he playing in his first match too.

His arm seemed to be serious from the very start. We knew it was broken. Aunty Mary, the school nurse, said so, but Patrick would have to go all the way to Ipoh for X-rays. Ipoh was over 70 miles away. You remember—we lived at the top of a mountain. The road down it snaked and curled for 40 of those miles.

A taxi was sent for. Aunty Mary settled Patrick as comfortably as she could, with a pillow under his head and a rug round him. Then she climbed in herself. The light was beginning to fade as we waved them round the bend in the drive. When would Patrick be back? I couldn't help wondering if he'd be all right. I thought of how sickening the journey could be even if you weren't in pain with a sore arm. I thought of his white face and closed eyes. I wished I could run and tell Mum, who would understand exactly how I felt. Oh, if only he had never been chosen for that match!

I left Stella playing ping-pong with Jill Peters and wandered up to the dorm. It was almost bath time. For the first time in my life I was undressed and ready before anyone else. I think Aunty Janet understood. She gave me a special hug that night and stayed whispering to me in the dark for an extra five minutes.

Patrick and Aunty Mary had to stay at Ipoh hospital overnight, but what a welcome they got on their arrival back next day!

'My arm, Toots,' he called as he bounded out of the taxi, 'it's fractured in two places!'

An admiring crowd began to gather. The plaster cast was so white and new! Patrick certainly looked like a wounded hero! Into the bargain, he couldn't tackle such subjects as English and Maths until he could write with his left hand!

My sympathy for Patrick began to wane!

And then there were the signatures! No one before had ever sported an autographed arm! All sorts of hiero- glyphics decorated that plaster—Chinese signatures, Indian, Malay, all the western countries, and even a Japanese one. The Chinese names were our helpers in the kitchen at Chefoo. The Indian was our gardener, the Malay was our office secretary, but I never heard where the Japanese name came from. It must have been someone he met at the hospital in Ipoh.

I was dying to write my name too. Think how well it would have looked. I could have made it take up at least 10 centimetres—Teresa Olivia Odetta Thrower! But he wouldn't let me sign—no girls' names were allowed.

The novelty of the brand-new plaster cast lasted a week at the most. Then everybody forgot about it—everybody, that is, except Patrick. He got tired not being able to do his best in class, for he was oozing with brains. He got tired not being able to join in the P.E. lessons or swim in our little pool. He just got tired and bored of the whole thing.

After six weeks it still wasn't over. The long journey to Ipoh had to be repeated to have the plaster removed. Patrick's arm was doing well, but he needed physiotherapy in sick bay and a further check up at the hospital. And all because of a little accident.

Looking back on those days, I just can't help wondering why there weren't more incidents like that. I think of our tree house, the swings we fell from, the climbing bars, our energetic P.E. lessons, and the tall tree in the corner just asking to be mastered. Yet accidents were few.

As you know, I believe it's because God's angel is

there that accidents are few. But I'm not sure why there are *some*—Patrick's, for instance, I'm not sure why Aunty Mary had all that extra work and responsibility. I'm not sure, either, why Dad had to foot a huge hospital bill. Maybe a Christian forgot to pray for us all that day. I really *don't* know—do you?

Next to me I think the person most upset by the whole affair was little Blue Socks. He felt the blame lying heavily on his heart. One day he led his Malay school team up our drive, dressed in ordinary shorts. He knocked on Patrick's classroom door.

'Di-mana Patrick?' he asked. (Where is Patrick?)

'Saya ada hadiah untok Patrick.' (I have a present for Patrick.)

A quick white grin lit up his sad little brown face. Then from behind his back, he produced a large durian.

9

STITCHES

An audible gasp of horror rose from the Chefoo boys and girls in the front row. Pacing up and down nervously in the wings, I heard it quite distinctly. I stopped in my tracks. Although I was behind the scenes, I heard that the gasping had turned to a tittering and then—there was just no doubt about it—everyone suddenly burst out laughing.

I stood there, rooted to the platform, in my warm furry costume. The audience wasn't *meant* to laugh there. I gazed at them through a slit in the curtain. The hall was dark, but I could see enough to detect the wave of merriment that rippled through it.

The light from the stage caught Paul Carter's and Justyn Melville's faces. Those wretched boys—they were in stitches. They should know better. *They'd* seen the rehearsal. They knew this was a *serious* part in the play. What on earth had gone wrong?

And then Mr M's voice came across the stage in a forced, urgent whisper.

'Get that mouse off!'

The mouse!

My eyes fell to the floor where it should have lain, awaiting its entrance. It wasn't there! Realization dawned. The colour began to creep into my already hot cheeks.

Uncle Ted was prompter and chief dresser-upper.

Thankful that no one could see me, I bent and pulled the string, retrieving Mouse from the centre of the stage where it had appeared far too early and in the wrong scene!

It had all been a matter of tripping over the cord unawares and releasing Mouse too soon. Great Scott! Had I ruined our Chefoo play? Nervousness forgotten, I began to think of what Mr M, our producer, would say afterwards. But I hadn't time to think.

'Puss, puss, where *are* you?' It was Uncle Ted. He was prompter and chief dresser-upper. '*Toots*—it's *you*. Get on, girl!'

Just in time I slid in to say my next part. It was my favourite bit where I laid down the law about what should be done with the ogre. The words came tumbling out. I needn't have been nervous after all. I needn't even have paced up and down. In fact, Mouse need never have appeared! I finished my speech and slinkily slid into the wings again. Uncle Ted was there.

'Good girl!' he whispered. 'Listen, they're clapping you!'

A sense of tremendous well-being, pride and pleasure rushed over me. I *loved* acting. The night of our school play was *the* night of my life, I thought. 'Puss in Boots'— was there ever a better play? Was there ever a better performance? I was thrilled with *every*thing.

As the residents of Tanah Rata melted out into the starry tropical night, we gathered in the dressing room for a treat of delicious eats, specially for the cast.

Everyone was talking, thirteen to the dozen, eyes bright, full of the tingly expectancy of Christmas.

And then the moment we were waiting for arrived. The Head came in to give us his comments. He needn't have said anything, though, for we *knew* he was pleased.

Grinning, he gave us a thumbs-up signal and said we deserved every mince pie Aunty Anna had in the freezer! Pity Aunty Anna wasn't there to hear it.

It was bony Jimmy Martin who brought up the subject of Mouse. I held my breath and almost choked on a chocolate swiss-roll crumb.

'I nearly hit high doh when I saw it,' Uncle Ted exploded. Then he started to guffaw and inside half a second we were all doubled up with him—even the Head!

'It was the funniest thing I've ever seen in my life,' gasped Mr M. 'There was Stella giving her pretty princess speech. There was old Hank ogling beautifully at her, and then suddenly this thing, this piece of brown blanket with whiskers on it, slid right into centre front!'

All over again we started to giggle.

'It's all very well laughing now,' grinned Stella, 'At the time I thought the audience was laughing at me!'

It was a good moment to confess my faults. I pushed back my whiskered head and explained what had happened. Nobody seemed to mind! Uncle Ted simply slapped me on the back and made me choke on another crumb.

That was Drama Club. What super fun! Clubs were great—Photography, where they went into the Dark Room to see what would develop; Junk Club; Brownies; Cub Scouts, and quite a host of others.

We were only allowed to join two, and Drama was my first choice. I had a hard time deciding about No. 2. Art with Uncle Ted? No, eventually I knew I must give in to the urge to create something with wool!

And in Crochet Club they were going to make ponchos. I simply had to have a poncho. Ponchos were the *in* thing at Chefoo. I could just visualize myself in one, and I liked the thought!

The whole idea was possible because of a huge box of new wool that had arrived at Chefoo as a gift. Oh, the thought of milling through those lovely coloured grams! Before I had my practice squares done, I had dreamed of me dressed in ponchos of about six different shades.

While listening to dear old Cliff on Mrs M's stereo, we all mastered the doubles, trebles and shells. Then we were off! I started the nicest poncho you have ever seen—pale blue and navy, designed from a cushion cover. I loved it from the very first chain. I'm glad I didn't know then that I was never to wear it.

Most of the girls in our dorm were in Crochet Club. As the days wore on towards Christmas and the end of term in Level 5, we used to gather round Aunty Kay in the evenings for a good-night story and in a cosy huddle the hooks would click in and out.

Aunty Kay was reading C. S. Lewis's *The Last Battle*. We were absolutely wrapped up in it. Nobody wanted to leave our sit-around and the warm atmosphere of home-liness, to climb into bed.

All sorts of dodges were tried to keep Aunty Kay from tucking us up. Questions usually won. She just *had* to answer, and by the time she had, someone else thought up another!

'It's super being in the top dorm at last,' breathed Fish, in the silence after the story one night.

'What do you like best about it?' invited Aunty Kay.

'Growing Up Club!' several of us chimed in quickly.

'In one way it's nice to grow up but sometimes I think it's just horrible,' I said.

'Why?'

'Well, pretty soon you have got to leave Chefoo. I don't fancy school at home.'

'At least you have got another year and a bit,' put in Stella. 'How'd you like to be me?'

I wished I'd never said anything. It had brought up the only thing I was finding hard to take this term—Stella was going home. You see, every four years or so our parents got leave and Stella's turn had come up. My own parents' leave had been postponed as Dad had been made Superintendent in North Thailand. It suited them to wait until I had finished Level 6. But I couldn't bear the thought of Chefoo without Stella.

That was the worst of Chefoo—you just got to love someone and then they were whisked eight thousand miles away from you.

In the glow of Aunty Kay's lamp, I gave Stella's arm a loving squeeze. If only *she* could stay and *Fish* leave. In the lamplight I stared at them both—Stella, slight, fair, pretty, good natured, and full of common sense, my own special friend. And Abigail Fischer, plump, waddly, a chewer of hair, and rotten tempered. As the rest of us worked at our ponchos, Stella was trying to knit a tie for her Dad. Fish did nothing, except chew. Neither Stella nor Fish had got into Crochet Club. I didn't care about Fish—she had Jewellery Club to make up—but Stella so longed to do a poncho too. Mrs M said it wasn't worth while Stella joining, as she was leaving so soon. I sighed.

'One nice thing,' said Stella, 'we're stopping off in Switzerland on the way home. We'll be in the French-speaking quarter and I'm going to practise my French.'

'My brother had to have a go at his French last year,'

chirped up Jill Peters. 'A group from his school went over to France for their Easter holidays.'

'How nice,' Aunty Kay put in hurriedly. I expect she saw us sitting there all night, travelling over the world in our imaginations! She began to make a few definite moves prior to getting us all off to bed.

Jill wasn't to be put off. 'Living in France is expensive,' she continued. 'Mum said we all had to save like mad to give my brother the chance to go. He needed lots of pocket money. You know, he was saving fran . . .'

Francs!

Jill bit her lip. Suddenly there was dead silence in the dorm. It was the sort of silence you can almost feel. Stella stopped knitting. I paused in my crochet, hook in mid-air. Fish actually pushed her hair out of her mouth and Aunty Kay stopped making going-to-bed movements.

The unfinished word hung in the air. '*Francs.*'

Every one of us must have thought the same thing at the same time. Jill looked at us. She knew what we were thinking and she burst into tears.

I watched what Aunty Kay would do. A crisis. But Jill's sobbing couldn't be ignored. Aunty Kay stood to her feet to lead her away to her own private room but Jill burst out, 'Okay then, *I* did it. Now you all know. It was for my brother. It wasn't for me. Anyhow you got it back, so stop staring at me, Colette. It must have fallen from under my pillow on to the floor.'

Aunty Kay gently led poor Jill down the floor of the dorm. The door closed on them. We knew we were meant to get quietly ready for bed, but we were quite thunder-struck. Jill Peters! Quiet little Jill had taken Colette's franc.

'Mean little beast,' grumped Fish. 'Now, Teresa Thrower, perhaps you'll believe at last that I did *not* add that franc to my coin collection.'

I said nothing. I should have, I know. But I didn't, not even when Colette prettily took me by the arm and apologized for thinking I ever had it.

The usual noisy chatter was rather hushed up that night, in the circumstances. After we had climbed into our bunks and the lights were out, Aunty Kay came to see if Colette was asleep. Then the two of them tip-toed down to the door. Several minutes later a sniffing Jill and a smug Colette came back. I suppose she apologized to her.

'Wonders'll never cease,' I thought. 'Imagine that mystery being cleared up at last.'

Leaning out of bed, I gently pulled the curtain back—just a fraction. Chefoo was dark and peaceful but my own thoughts were all mixed up. They switched in a terrible triangle from one idea to another:

1 We knew who took the French franc.
2 Jill had apologized to Colette. Colette had apologized to me. Yet I couldn't bring myself to say sorry to Abigail Fischer. It looked as if this hatred was going to master me for life. I still couldn't manage to live like a Christian.
3 Stella was leaving. Dear Stella. Emotionally I thought of how much I loved her. What could I give her as a goodbye present?

The days crept on towards the end of the term. Everything would have been wonderful except for Stella going. This time she would not set off at midnight with me on the long trip to Thailand. She was going to meet her parents in Singapore.

That last Sunday we spent a lot of time together. We sat on the bench outside the dorm, in turn whispering, in turn quiet.

'Stella,' I said at last. Our time was almost gone. 'Stella, I've got something for you. It's a goodbye present. Something special—for you.'

I dashed into the dorm, and came out with a carefully-wrapped, soft and lumpy parcel.

'With lots of love,' I said chokily, as I pushed it towards her.

She stared, unbelieving.

'What is it?'

'Open it,' I instructed. 'Try it on.'

'But I can't take this!' she gasped at last.

'I want you to have it.'

'But . . . all that work! Dear old Toots, how will I ever thank you?'

'It looks lovely on you,' I said, eyes shining with the pleasure of giving.

And it did. Stella MacAlpine, my best friend ever, looked beautiful in my gorgeous navy and pale blue, tasselled poncho.

10

REMEMBER JESUS CHRIST

'Teresa Thrower. Britain and North Thailand.' Mr Canning's voice thundered in my ears. Miss Fletcher struck up *God save the Queen*. I took a deep breath, gathered up the folds of my long skirt in my hands, and stepped forward.

The music, our teacher's voice, the crowded assembly hall, the Head's upright presence—I felt dizzy with the grandeur of it all as I found my place on the platform among all my other classmates.

It was Graduation Day at Chefoo. I'd never looked or felt as grand in all my life. Aunty Kay had done my hair up in a huge bow behind my head. As I had taken a quick glance in the dorm mirror she'd said, 'Toots Thrower, you're growing up!'

So, here we sat on the platform of the school assembly hall. I found myself in the same old spot where Mouse had made his early entrance. And now, here was another great occasion.

Looking down at the little kids in the front, I wondered if I could ever have been as small as that, at Chefoo. A quick smile played on my lips as I remembered Aunty Eva's introduction to me. Wasn't it too bad about her poor shoes!

The smile disappeared. I could see Patrick halfway down the hall. Patrick—my young brother, broken arm long ago forgotten, the boy who was already Chefoo's soccer hero. He was growing up too. Being in a place of honour on the platform today meant goodbye to Patrick. I pushed the thought away. This was a day for laughter, not tears. I didn't want to think of separation from Patrick just then.

And there was next year's top class—right at the back of the room now. I remembered when I'd been in their place last year. The leaving Level Sixers had seemed so grown-up, so important—and now I was one of them.

Giving myself a little shake, I dragged my thoughts back to the present. The Head was giving a thumb-nail sketch of each one of us. I blushed crimson when he came to me.

'Toots Thrower,' he said, 'is the most enthusiastic girl we've ever had at Chefoo. Loving or hating, Toots does it with her whole heart! This enthusiasm has given great rewards in her school work. Her best subject is English. I can imagine her fitting very well into the world of journalism. She also makes a very good Puss in Boots.'

Everyone laughed! The Head had chosen out the nice things to say about each of us. For instance, he never mentioned my Maths—good job! That other bit, about loving and hating—I'd have to think that out!

One by one we were called out to receive our Diplomas—rectangles of paper, tied with red ribbon, that became very precious.

THIS IS TO CERTIFY THAT

TERESA OLIVIA ODETTA THROWER
has successfully completed
her primary education
at

Chefoo School, Cameron Highlands,
Pen. Malaysia

REMEMBER JESUS CHRIST

J. J. Melville
Headmaster

That evening we had a banquet—a *banquet*, not a party. What a feast! I was only sorry that Stella had gone home, over a year ago now, and couldn't join in.

Level 6 had been hard without Stella, but yet it was full of more interests and activities than we'd ever experienced before.

As we were being educated in Malaysia, the teachers thought we should go home with some knowledge of that colourful land. So it came about that our class set off with Mr Canning to Kuala Lumpur for a week-long class trip.

Mind you, we'd had class trips before. We'd visited a rubber plantation and a tin mine in Level 5, and we'd seen tea and oil palm in Level 4—but they had only been *day* trips. That week in Kuala Lumpur was quite something.

The Overseas Missionary Fellowship Guest Home in Kuala Lumpur was brave enough to cater for us for the week. Visits in the morning, school in the afternoon. Even with the temperature in the nineties, we had a super time.

What do you think of this poem, written by Hank Barrows after our morning at the zoo?

A CAMEL RIDE

I got on a two-humped camel
What an interesting mammal!
Whoosh, up he rose,
I was flung towards his nose!
I came down with a little thump,
And settled in front of the hump.
The camel moved at the sound of command,
I held on with my legs and hand.
Soon the camel stopped and did a little cough
I felt like getting off.
But suddenly the camel kneeled down with a smack.
Scared, inside me, I climbed off his back.
That was the best ride I ever had.
And I was glad!

And this was composed by Jill Peters:

THE CHIMP

A big black chimp
Came out with a limp,
As black as ink
But its bottom was pink!
I frowned
And with one bound
He was away.
Round and chubby,
Like a lump of clay!

So you see, the school part wasn't too bad. No Maths at all, all week. Just English and making scrap books. We went to the Houses of Parliament, a Batek factory, the lovely modern Oriental museum and, of course, that fantabulous visit to the zoo.

It wouldn't be possible ever to forget Chefoo with memories like these. My head was full of memories. My thoughts dashed from Kuala Lumpur back to the Camerons. Through the windows of the dining hall, I could just see the jungle, the shadowy, forbidden jungle where John had got his snake bite. Beyond it was the valley where the stream flowed—the stream that led to Pete's pasture and his burial ground.

I forced my blurred vision away. On the other side I knew the jungled mountains were scarred with long, orange, sandy wounds, telling the story of landslides. I remembered a day at Chefoo when the sky *wasn't* bright with puffy clouds, and the cruel mountain had tumbled into the classroom.

Classrooms! Dear old classrooms where we learnt to write—italic style for me, because I was from Britain, but I had imbibed some American longhand and a few Australian squiggles too. Friendly old classroom where Colette's franc had disappeared at decimal currency time.

I needn't think badly of Jill, though. Hadn't my own conscience been stirred in that Post Box assembly? When was that—surely not two years ago? And I'd done nothing about it yet. Quickly I brushed that disturbing thought away.

Isn't it hard, though, when *one* memory tries to spoil all the nice ones? Sometimes lying in bed at night I'd take time to think—think really deeply, that is.

I loved Chefoo School life except for one thing. I guess you know it. Fish.

Two years since I'd been challenged at assembly about loving your enemies. Stubbornly I'd refused to love Fish. And then, of course, as you know, I felt I wasn't a Christian.

So I'd lie and think about it all. When I was honest, I knew I wanted to live like a Christian. That would mean saying sorry to God, but I knew that was no use if I couldn't apologize to Fish. This hatred of my enemy had grown into a huge barrier between the Lord Jesus and me.

Somehow I knew I had to put this right before I left Chefoo.

I struggled and struggled inside. I persuaded myself that I didn't know how to go about making things right. I believed Fish would laugh at me if I tried to say something nice to her. I just kept putting it off.

By Graduation Day I was still putting it off. Not much time was left now. Just two weeks.

And then the Head had said that thing about loving *and* hating. I'm sure he didn't mean to hit me for six! The speeches were all so nice and complimentary. It was just that I realized it was true—I *was* an enthusiastic hater.

That night, after the banquet, I could hear it all again, in my mind, as I lay in bed in the quiet darkness of the dorm. Usually I fell asleep very quickly but tonight. . . . 'Loving or hating, Toots does it with her whole heart. . . . Do something nice for your enemy today.'

I almost sat up in bed.

Where had that second sentence come from? I could clearly hear it singing in my ears as though it was tacked on to the Graduation speech. It was the advice we'd received at assembly that day over two years ago, but I'd never taken any notice of it.

Suddenly that night I knew this was my answer. My wakeful, energetic mind started to think of something nice I could do for Fish before it was too late.

Ends of terms are always very busy. This year I'd not only be packing my case for the holidays but my trunk for going, too. I was going away—for ever. This year I'd not be putting my note books in the next classroom. They'd come home, too—for ever.

I became horribly gloomy about it all. But so did we all. Somehow we began to think we'd never really appreciated Chefoo till that moment. Had we really taken everything for granted?

The last school day dawned—sunny and bright as usual in the Cameron Highlands. Half-past two found the school gathered in the hall for our final assembly.

Awards were presented, the top class was prayed for, staff going on leave were remembered, a taped message from our School Director in Singapore was played, and the Head gave a short goodbye talk.

'I'll not say "Remember Chefoo",' he told us. 'I know you will. But it's more important to know Chefoo's motto, "Remember Jesus Christ". That is the thing which can make your life for you. Whether you remember *Him* or not can determine your success or failure.'

Remember Jesus Christ! I'd had enough Bible teaching to know what Jesus was like. I knew, for instance, how *He*

'I'll not say "Remember Chefoo",' he told us. . . . 'It's more important to know Chefoo's motto.'

would treat an enemy. It would be—as a friend. A friend, perhaps like Stella?

'Gail,' I called, forcing gaiety into my voice as we ran out of the assembly hall.

I think she nearly dropped when I used her proper name!

'Gail,' I persevered, 'can you come to the dorm a moment? I've got something for you. It's a goodbye present.'

I could see she didn't believe me. I knew I'd have to go further.

'Gail, it's to say I'm sorry for the big number of times I've been rude to you, and especially I'm sorry for accusing you about the French franc.'

I gulped. Gail was still looking very surprised.

'Stay there,' I commanded, pushing her on to the same bench where Stella and I had said our goodbyes. I ran quickly to the dorm.

This present was wrapped too. I'd prepared it well in advance. It also was large, lumpy and soft.

'There,' I said, 'it's to show I mean the sorries. Open it.'

Gail tore off the coloured paper. I could see she was terribly pleased. She held up my long crocheted dachshund that I'd spent this term making at Crochet Club. It was meant to be for keeping the draught out from under the door of our little shack in North Thailand; but I knew this was a better use.

Do you know what Gail did? She hugged me. All had been made well.

And now, here I am—twelve years old, and Chefoo is just a memory. School, so far from Mum and Dad, has had its bad moments, *very* bad, but I think the highlights of school life made up for those homesick times.

Today I am writing in Britain, because Mum and Dad are on leave this year. Next August they plan to return to North Thailand. I'll stay here, at boarding school in England, for my secondary education.

I'll stay here. They'll go back, with Patrick.

I'm really dreading being separated from them again. This time, there'll be *eight* thousand miles between us. Is it the right thing? Is taking the Good News about Jesus to the people in North Thailand worth it?

The only answer I can find is in a verse out of the Bible that Mum showed me—a very special verse.

'Let me assure you,' said Jesus, 'that no one has ever given up anything—home, brothers, sisters, mother, father, children or property—for love of me and to tell others the Good News, who won't be given back a hundred times over, homes, brothers, sisters, mothers, children and lands—with persecutions! All these will be his <u>here on earth</u> and in the world to come he shall have eternal life.'

I've underlined the bits that are important to me. This verse has come true for me, so far. You see, Chefoo *was* a hundred times better than any other school I could ever have gone to. From what I've written, I'm sure you'd agree with me. It just had so many extras—I'd need to write ten more chapters to explain them all.

And now? Dad says holiday times will be so special that they will help to make up for the times in between when we do get lonely.

I can't find any other answer than the one Jesus gave:

'No one has ever given up anything ... who won't be given back a hundred times over ... here on earth ... *and* eternal life.'